REACHING THE UNREACHED

*ICTs and Adult Education for the
Empowerment of Rural Women*

Olivia Adwoa Tiwaah Frimpong Kwapong

University Press of America,® Inc.
Lanham · Boulder · New York · Toronto · Plymouth, UK

DEDICATED TO ALL RURAL WOMEN

CONTENTS

1

INTRODUCTION

INTRODUCTION

The quest for global stability and peace has placed poverty reduction at the centre of research and policy deliberations. In the year 2000, the nations of the world declared the *Millennium Development Goals* (MDG's), consisting of a set of eight goals that directly address the problem of poverty alleviation. Seven of the eight goals – eradication of extreme poverty and hunger, universal primary education, gender equality and women's empowerment, reduction in child mortality, improvements in maternal health care, combating HIV/AIDS, malaria and other diseases, and environmental sustainability – are directly concerned with how carefully-formulated policies and programs can help to improve the overall well-being of women in society. The MDG's certainly highlight the central role of equity and opportunities for women in aiding world advancement (http://www.un.org/millenniumgoals.

Ghana is a signatory to the declaration of the MDG's, and has designed and implemented policies and programs directed toward poverty reduction and economic well-being. Ghana's poverty reduction program places women at the centre of policy initiatives because, as Awumbila points out, "Gender disparities exist and closing the gender gap and enhancing women's participation in development is essential not only for building a just society, but is also a pre-requisite for achieving political, social, economic, cultural and environmental security among people on a sustainable basis" (2001, 33).

Both the MDG's and Ghana's Poverty Reduction Strategy Program (GPRSP) recognize the disadvantaged situation of women, and in addressing the problem of poverty they emphasize the *empowering of women* as a specific goal. Both raise at least two broad issues: first, what is the content of empowerment programs, and second, in the designing and implementing of empowerment programs, how does society enlist the participation of the *population affected*? In terms of content, in designing women's empowerment programs the literature suggests that *information* is the key ingredient. *Empowerment* (a term promoted by Paulo Freire, the Brazilian radical educator) is a broad concept. From an educational perspective (and in a manner that suits the context of this study), UNESCO has defined Empowerment thusly:

> How individuals/communities engage in learning processes in which they create, appropriate and share knowledge, tools and techniques in order to change and improve the quality of their own lives and societies. Through empowerment, individuals not only manage and adapt to change but also contribute to/generate changes in their lives and environments. (www.unesco.org/ education /educprog /lwf /doc /portfolio /definitions.htm)

An extensive literature exists on the complex interactions and causal relationships between the various factors that go into defining empowerment. While information is clearly an important first stage in empowerment, it does not address the emotional or social dimensions involved, nor does it necessarily lead to changes in behaviour unless learning takes place based on the information.

The second broad issue, how to obtain the participation of the population affected by empowerment policies and programs, contains sub-issues, one of which is how can a developing economy like Ghana take advantage of modern ICT in support of empowering women in rural areas? The UN World Summit on the Information Society (WSIS)[1] Geneva, 2003, ICT defined ICT this way:

> The whole range of technologies designed to access, process and transmit information with regard to text, sound, data and pictures. ICT encompass the full range from traditional widely used devices such as radios, telephones or television to more sophisticated tools like computers or the Internet. (20)

This book adopts a simple definition of ICT as "the electronic means of capturing, processing, storing and communicating disseminating information" (www.neda.gov.ph/mtpdp2001/glossary_of_terms.htm).

There is considerable optimism that appropriate policies and programs regarding ICT and empowerment of rural women could yield great benefits to the country. A key conclusion drawn at the meeting of Ghana National Information Communication Technology Policy and Plan Development Committee and Women's Organizations was that "women could benefit greatly if they were empowered with the information communication technology." The Committee also agreed that information technology could be an effective tool for the political empowerment of women; for education and disseminating information and indigenous knowledge; and for strengthening women's participation in the political process (http://www.ict.gov.gh/html/women's%20organization.htm). There is also academic and research support for expanding the role of ICT in empowerment of rural women: "The potential link between knowledge and economic growth leads proponents of ICT for the developing world to argue that improved access to quality information can deliver tangible benefits to even the poorest of the world's poor" (Marclay 2001,1). In the light of national objectives, and given the new possibilities and the pace of change in ICT, there is an ongoing need for countries to assess the sustainability, investment, and cost implications of the changes

ICT'S AND WOMEN'S EMPOWERMENT

There is broad consensus that ICT could play an important role to make development effective on a large scale for disadvantaged people. For example, several resolutions of the UN General Assembly and statements by the UN Secretary-General Kofi Annan have endorsed the importance of ICT for development:

> "Over the last few years, a wide consensus has emerged on the potential of information and communications technologies (ICT) to promote economic growth, combat poverty, and facilitate the integration of developing countries into the global economy. Seizing the opportunities of the digital revolution is one of the most pressing challenges we face." (UN Secretary-General Kofi Annan, General Assembly 2002)

Also, countries in Sub-Sahara Africa (SSA) established the African Information Society Initiative (AISI) under Resolution 812 XXXI to "end Africa's information and information technology gap by bringing it into the Information Age." This is likely due to the growing concern as expressed by a notable scientist/scholar from Ghana;

> *We paid the price of not taking part in the Industrial Revolution of the late eighteenth century because we did not have the opportunity to see what was taking place in Europe. Now we see that information and communication technology has become an indispensable tool. This time, we should not miss out on this technological revolution.* Allotey 2000).

At the World Summit on Information Society (WSIS), in Geneva 2003 under the theme 'ICT4D' (Information and Communication for Development), ICT was defined to include: "The whole range of technologies designed to access, process and transmit information in regard to text, sound, data and pictures. ICT encompass the full range from traditional widely used devices such as radios, telephones or television to more sophisticated tools like computers or the Internet" (pg.20)

It was observed at the Summit that ICT's are part of the day-to-day reality of a rapidly increasing number of people everywhere. Information and communication technologies provide new opportunities for those who are literate, have good education and adequate resources. But because disadvantaged and marginalized groups have little chance to automatically benefit from ICT social divides are further increased and the   gap between rich and poor countries, regions, individuals and even between men and women is widens. The Summit concluded that for the poor the real issue is not whether ICT's are desirable because the technology is not even part of their broader context. The growing question of *bread or computers* is based on a mistaken understanding of ICT's role in and for development, yet provides a useful starting point for a debate on how ICT's can be effective tools for development and poverty reduction (http://www .itu.int/wsis/). The real issue is whether we accept that in addition to the existing deprivation of income, food and health services *the poor should be further deprived of new opportunities to improve their livelihoods and indeed, their lives.* The strategic choice is whether to accept the rapidly growing gap caused by a very asymmetric architecture of opportunities or whether to use ICT in a creative ways in order to level the playing field in economic, social, cultural and political terms.

Closely linked to the debate on the digital revolution is a new emphasis of the World Bank on *Knowledge for Development* and the *Knowledge Economy* which points to the success of the *New Economy* as a core process for world development.
The establishment of the UN ICT Task Force is another important step toward drawing attention to the global importance of ICT. At the WSIS was a strong presence and involvement where developing countries demonstrated the overall importance which the developing world attaches to ICT as its Platform demonstrated the enormous potential, the capacities and concrete programs in using ICT for development

Ghana has responded to the ICT challenge. In 2003, Ghana announced the *Ghana Integrated ICT for Accelerated Development* (ICT4AD) *Policy* which summarized the vision of Ghana in the Information Age. While the policy outlines a broad array of objectives, it is clear that the essential part of the policy is to use ICT to achieve Ghana's vision of becoming a middle-income country by the year 2020 (Ghana Vision 2020 – the First Steps). Ghana's ICT policy is supported by numerous supporting laws, programs and initiatives, such as the National Initiative Concerning the ICT and Education and Training (NISI), the African Information Society Initiative (AISI), and the Science and
Technology Policy Research Institute.

There is considerable optimism that appropriate policies and programs regarding ICT and empowerment of rural women could yield great benefits to the country. A key conclusion drawn at the meeting of Ghana National Information Communication Technology Policy and Plan Development Committee and Women's Organizations was that "women could benefit greatly if they were empowered with the information communication technology." The Committee also agreed that information technology could be an effective tool for the political empowerment of women; education disseminating information and indigenous knowledge; and strengthening women's participation in the political process (http://www.ict.gov.gh/html/ women's%20organization.htm). There is also academic and research support for expanding the role of ICT in empowerment of rural women. As mentioned by Marclay (2001), "The potential link between knowledge and economic growth leads proponents of ICT for the developing world to argue that improved access to quality information can deliver tangible benefits to even the poorest of the world's poor" (http://edevelopment. media.mit.edu/SARI/papers/pae.ksg.pdf). The FAO acknowledges that ICT's can be used as tools to empower women with the technological information and skills necessary for sustainable food security and livelihood. New information and communication technologies hold a unique opportunity for women in the developing world to speak out, be more visible and less isolated and hence support their increased political, social and economic participation at every level (<http://www.fao.org/sd/ruralradio/ en/ index.html≥).

TARGETING ADULT EDUCATION AND ICT'S FOR POVERTY REDUCTION AMONG RURAL WOMEN

Adult education has been most currently and briefly described in the Encarta Reference Library (2005) as: "All forms of schooling and learning programs in which adults participate." It is further explained that, unlike other forms of education, adult education is defined by the student population rather than by the content or complexity of a learning program. It includes both formal and non-formal educational programmes like literacy training, community development, on-the-job training, university credit programs and continuing professional education. Programs vary in organization from casual, incidental learning to formal college credit courses. Institutions offering education to adults include colleges, libraries, museums, social services, non-governmental and governmental agencies, businesses and churches (Encarta 2005).

A person's desire to participate in an educational program is often the result of a changing personal, social or vocational situation. This individual orientation has resulted in the creation of a continually changing and dynamic field able to respond to the varied needs of society. Recognizing the need to update information and skills, the desire for knowledge and information is also increasing among women. Rapidly changing technical fields also require constant updating of information in order for workers to remain effective and productive.

In Ghana, as a result of the limited educational opportunities in the formal school system voluntary adult education associations emerged as far back as 1830s. In an effort to keep abreast of the times and improve upon their educational standards, these associations engaged in discussions and implementation of literacy programmes. Some also wanted further studies for promotion and salary increment. Through this process, adult education in Ghana has progressed to the University level to provide both formal and non-formal education to the masses (Amedzro 2005)

As explained in Encarta (2005), another major development in information communication in adult education is the increasing use of radio, network television and cable television for educating adults. Broadcast media are being used worldwide to provide public information, teach reading and writing, and specialized seminars and short courses as well as providing university-degree programs. With millions of personal computers and videocassette recorders in use, helping adults learn via these non-broadcast technologies is growing rapidly. These electronic media offer the means for reaching populations that are geographically isolated or homebound like those in rural communities in Ghana.

A literate population is a necessity for any nation wishing to take advantage of modern technological growth. Research has shown a direct relationship between literacy among women and improved health and child care in the family. The United Nations Educational, Scientific and Cultural Organization (UNESCO) encouraged literacy programs, agricultural extension and community instruction. In *New Technologies for Literacy and Adult Education: a Global Perspective,* Wagner and Kozima (2003), of the International Literacy Institute – National Centre on Adult Literacy University of Pennsylvania, discuss the interface between information technologies and adult education and explain the need for a refined concept of adult education that meets the needs of the 21st Century and takes advantage of technology opportunities. The authors share two approaches by which technology could improve literacy and for that matter, women's empowerment. The authors defined ICT as "a set of potential delivery and instructional tools that can be used to help people acquire the skills associated with the traditional notions of literacy" (15).

Wagner and Kozma's view of the role of ICT in adult education is built around the premise that literacy, technology and development must be considered as an integrated set of tools. The first of the two approaches the authors identified for using ICT's to promote literacy is to use capabilities of technology to deliver instruction in support of cognitive skills required to read and understand text. To a large extent, this approach echoes the functional literacy approach. The second approach which is mainly on medium of delivery focuses on how technology can be used to efficiently support the use of text and developing literacy skills for distance learning when instruction and other resources are not available.

There is tremendous potential for using its and adult education to empower rural women. Other major problems facing rural women's access to training and educational opportunities include distance, poor road networks and infrastructural development. Considering the inaccessibility of rural locations, the deprived nature of rural communities and the potential of Information and Communication Technologies for reaching the unreached in society, one comprehends the need to explore new and innovative information technology in the promotion of adult learning among rural women. Some new technologies identified include solar powered radios and televisions, *Leapfrog*'s talking book, cell phone devices and pocket computers/Personal Digital Assistant (PDA) (Kwapong 2005). Appropriate technologies for household chores, food processing, preservation and storage and farm tools that are appropriate for women increase productivity and save time for studies and small transportation equipment which will free women from head loading are also required.

Harnessing the potential of ICT's would obviously help bridge the rural / urban and gender divide. The shift in development thinking and practice towards people-centred programmes and the participation of people and communities in decisions concerning their own lives is creating new opportunities for social change and the empowerment of both women and men in rural areas. This shift is vital to stimulate their awareness, involvement and capabilities further.

Different methods of communication and media could facilitate development by encouraging dialogue and debate. They can give a voice to rural women, thus enabling them to formulate and articulate their own development agendas. By fostering the exchange of knowledge and information, communication can stimulate women's awareness and motivation, allowing them to make informed decisions on the crucial issues affecting their lives.

Communication can also promote changes in attitudes and social behaviours and help communities to identify sustainable opportunities and development solutions that are within their reach. In addition to putting development planners in a position to respect women's traditional knowledge, communication processes can improve the management and effectiveness of new social organizations and institutions, ensuring that they provide services to women in a participatory and democratic manner. When used effectively, communication acts as a mediation tool between planners and rural communities, helping to resolve conflicts, achieve consensus and find common ground for policies and actions to be taken. Media and communication technologies can be powerful tools for advising women about new ideas and practices and improving training and help rural women to exchange experiences and learn from each other. Communication has been identified as the key to raising awareness, sharing knowledge and supporting a broader debate on indigenous knowledge and biodiversity, all of which are conducive to more effective policies and action programs. The majority of rural women are illiterate and live in remote, isolated areas where access to information, lack of transportation, a scarcity of trainers and cultural and language differences are common problems. The use of appropriate communication technologies will obviously help to address such problems.

The communication technologies and expertise already exist. The challenge now is to use them appropriately and effectively in ways that give a voice to rural women and promote social change and sustainable agricultural and rural development for both women and men. In this process, adult learning approaches must be explored. As far back as the 1984 FAO Consultation, communication experts indicated that people-oriented and sustainable development can only realize its full potential if rural people are involved and motivated and information and knowledge are shared. As adult educational approaches enforce, sharing is not a one-way transfer of information; it implies an exchange between communications equals. Conversely, technical specialists learn about people's needs and their techniques of production; on the other, the people learn about the techniques and proposals of the specialists. This means that participatory communication efforts with rural women should begin with development planners and technical specialists listening to them. Listening goes beyond a simple appraisal of needs. It involves listening to what women already know, what they aspire to become, what they perceive as possible and desirable and what they feel they can sustain. Although often illiterate, rural women have wisdom, knowledge and practices based on deep-rooted cultural norms, traditions and values, as well as generations of experience. This indigenous knowledge should be taken into account, respected, valued and traditional methods of information exchange and communication should be coupled   with modern means.

Communication strategies and materials should reflect women's perceptions, needs and perspectives. The use of participatory and qualitative research methods such as participatory rural appraisal (PRA) focus group discussions, interpersonal communication techniques and audiovisual media help to generate qualitative data. It also helps to enable communication specialists and communities to quicken the process of sharing experiences and learning together. Where the questionnaire and statistical surveys were once the main tools of research and analysis, there now exists a mix of methods that are not dependent on literacy and formal education capabilities that can be applied to discover the problems and needs of rural women as well as the opportunities and solutions open to the community.

For effective use of ICT's for empowerment of rural women, communication efforts will have to begin with development planners listening to women and carefully considering their perceptions and needs, their knowledge and experience and their culture and traditions. Planners must also take into account the reality of rural areas and the changes required to improve the livelihoods of rural women in ways that can be accepted and sustained.

A holistic approach will also have to be adopted. Thus, communication efforts should cover all the multifaceted aspects of life which affect women in rural areas including agriculture; the environment; health sanitation family planning; education and literacy. A holistic approach should be used to ensure that women's concerns are integrated into research and extension programmes. Success in achieving sustainable and equitable development is increasingly dependent on the acquisition of information and knowledge.

A multi channel approach is also crucial here. Communication programmes need to make use of all available modern and traditional media infrastructure and channels within each country so that appropriate technologies and media could be applied according to the prevailing cultural, social and economic conditions. Programmes have to be participatory and interactive. Special attention has to be given to the communication channels most suited to women. If approached in these ways, training programmes for rural women which explore the strength of modern technology will help bridge the existing divides. (Balit 1999).

Harnessing the potential of emerging technologies to address the issue of world poverty through adult education was recognized at 2004 International Conference of Adult Education, and focused on poverty reduction. Among its recommendation for action was the call to lobby for financial support for all levels of adult education in recognition that basic literacy education is not enough for poverty reduction and that people living in poverty also need continuous training and access to relevant technologies. Recognizing the poverty situation of rural women and the potentials of information technologies for women's empowerment, the observations and proposals at the Conference highlighted the usefulness of adult education for empowerment of rural women.

CONCLUSION

Technological advancement is ongoing and here to stay, and has tremendous potential for bridging the rural-urban divide and the gender gap. Harnessing these potentials in a developing country like Ghana comes with a lot of institutional and infrastructural challenges. The existing institutional and infrastructural challenges that accompany the use of information technologies do not prevent one from looking for alternative policy options. In developing a credible and sustainable ICT policy to empower rural women, one will likely have to consider the socio-economic characteristics of households, including the degree of determination of their willingness to pay for alternative ICT technologies.

In addition, recognizing the potentials of adult education for human resource development, the International Conference of Adult Education [ICAE, 2004] recommends the use of adult education for poverty reduction at all levels and advocates the use of relevant technologies in this process as well.

NOTE

1. The World Summit on the Information Society (WSIS) is a UN summit in two phases, the first in Geneva in 2003, the second in Tunis in 2005. The International Telecommunication Union (ITU) has the lead for the WSIS. WSIS has stimulated a worldwide debate and increased awareness about the transition to the information society. It helped to put ICT for development high on the international agenda of burning issues. http://www.itu.int/wsis/

2
SITUATION OF RURAL WOMEN

INTRODUCTION

It has been internationally acknowledged that rural women have been key actors in solving the major issues on the development agenda, including the need to manage the environment in a sustainable manner, the exploding rate of population and urbanization, food security, human health needs, education and literacy and the elimination of poverty. Globally, women produce more than half the food that is grown and are primarily responsible for preparing, storing and processing food. In rural areas the total work day is 20% longer as compared to urban areas. Women in rural areas spend an average of 20% more time than men working. In urban areas they spend 6% more time (Human Development Report, 1995). The feminization of agriculture has placed a considerable burden on women's capacity to produce, provide and prepare food in the face of already considerable social, economic and cultural constraints. Civil strife, rural-urban migration of men in search of employment and the growing number of mortalities attributed to HIV/AIDS have led to an increase in female-headed households in the developing world. Despite their essential role in achieving global food security, household, community and societal development, the contributions of rural women are often underestimated and overlooked when creating and developing strategies. Subsequently, they often remain "invisible" partners in the development process. From the 1970's to date, there has been interaction and knowledge building to move the focus on women in agricultural and rural development from the margins to centre stage. Meanwhile mainstreaming women's issues in development strategies continues to be hindered by limited capacity and commitment within development agencies and national governments (Balit 1999). However, the empowerment of rural women through the exchange of knowledge and information is crucial for enhancing rural living conditions and achieving development goals.

INVISIBILITY

Though they play a major role in the rural area, rural women suffer invisibility and marginalization, and their contributions are underappreciated in relation to that of men. Rural women hold a central position in the production of food at the world level, which reaches 80% in African countries, 60% in Asian countries and 30-40% in the South. They have an important place in rural labour but are hardly ever acknowledged as producers or given the responsibility for the management of natural resources utilized in their productive work. Since they are mainly the ones in charge of housework, women play a vital role in a rural home's economy, and they are their main guarantee of survival. This contribution, which systematically implies double working hours, often remains unnoticed. The proportion of the female population who are economically active in the rural sector is up to five times more than the figures registered in official surveys and censuses indicates that rural women suffer from statistical invisibility as well. Lack of gender-desegregated data from rural areas prevents policymakers from including women's' concerns in development programmes while women farmers' wealth of accumulated experience and knowledge often passes unnoticed. Meanwhile, accurate gender information is crucial in the formulation of agricultural development and food security strategies.

Generally, society, and even rural women themselves, has greatly undervalued and often completely ignored the role of women in maintaining and developing the living countryside with its rich and diversified heritage and traditions. Too little has been done to fully recognise and appreciate their role on farms and in rural communities; legally, economically, technologically and statistically.

Full recognition of women's role in rural development would greatly contribute to rural prosperity and would help usher in sustainable rural development in the poorer countries and regions of the world. Planners and policy-makers need accurate information regarding women's' actual contribution to agriculture, and their potential to demonstrate a spirit of solidarity and cooperation with other rural women's events around the World. It was therefore proposed at the celebration of the 2005 World's Rural Women's Day, that the World should publicize the contribution of rural and farming women in all areas annually on October 15. The main purpose of the World Rural Women's Day was to bring rural women out of obscurity at least once a year to remind society how much they owe to rural women and to give value and credit to their work (UNESCO 2001; UN 2005a; UN 2005b). Efforts at creating awareness about the work of rural women will help to inform the whole world about their contribution and seek support for their efforts.

RURAL WOMEN AND AGRICULTURE

Statistics confirm that almost 70% of the economically active women work in the rural sector. It has been internationally observed that rural women make a tremendous contribution to agriculture. The vast majority of the poor on our planet live in rural areas and 70% of these poor are women and their main resource is farming. They produce both food and cash crops. Today, female farmers are the majority of the 1,500 million people who live in absolute poverty (ILO 2003). A more recent study reveals that rural women currently make up 65.6% of agricultural labour (Yuan 2003). Recent statistics provided by FAO (2005) on the celebration of the 2005 World Rural Women's Day also indicate that the number of rural women (mainly farmers) total at least 1.6 billion and represent more than a quarter of the total world population. Women produce on average more than half of all the food that is grown: up to 80% in Africa, 60% in Asia and between 30 and 40% in Latin America and Western countries. In most sub-Saharan African countries, women make a significant contribution to food production and to the processing and marketing of foodstuffs as well. Since more rural men are migrating to urban areas to find a better standard of living, rural women have not only become the mainstay of their families, but also of farming. Meanwhile, it has been reported that their role in agriculture is not fully recognised. Only 5% of all agricultural extension resources are directed toward women. In low income countries with food deficits, this disparity is even more noticeable and shows a clear correspondence between women and poverty which acquires dramatic proportions in rural areas. When female farmers' access to the means of production is reduced, the number of people suffering from poverty and its direct consequences (hunger, malnutrition, disease and death) rises inescapably. Furthermore, the overload of work women suffer is reflected in a sharp rise in child labour and an increase in school dropout. Rural women lack access to technology and support in old age. In many cases they do not benefit from a social security system since they are classed as farmers' wives. The over-exploitation of women's labour traditionally results in an inequality of the salaries for equivalent work and competence. In spite of the noticeable increase of the participation of women in the world of labour in the past few years, this difference in the recognition of labour in the farming sector still persists (UN 2005a; UN 2005b).

Rural women in Africa, especially Sub-Saharan Africa, also face formidable obstacles to their potential role as a major economic and social force in the development of the agricultural sector in their countries. There is the concern that these issues affecting rural women in agriculture are not taken into account in policies and this has a strong consequence in the expected results. It could lead to an increase in women's work load, affect the health of both women and children who provide labour and possibly a complete waste of their contributions and abilities (Manuh 1998); FAO 2005; ILO 2003).

The situation of rural women in agriculture makes it necessary to adopt a systematic gender perspective in the assessment of development processes as

proposed in the gender mainstreaming approach. This could be done at the diag-
nostic stage of the original situation and throughout the phases and modes of
intervention in order to ensure effectiveness, quality and sustainability in the
actions undertaken. The contribution of women to agricultural and rural development could be maximized by implementing solutions to the specific problems
they encounter. An alternative strategy is to take women's know-how into account in a participatory approach. Attention will also have to be paid to the economic dimension of women's work in rural areas. This includes entrepreneurial
factors which are directly related to rural employment and the economy, and
their social, economic and legal implications. Credit provision decentralisation
(which brings decision-making to the local level and hence to women and affirmative action policies) has been shown to enhance the position of rural
women in agriculture and other areas of operation.

Labour is also a bottleneck for female farmers as men have left rural
economies in search of more viable livelihoods. Women have lost access to
male help on farms and to the money they may have previously provided. In
countries like Lesotho, Botswana and Burkina Faso, the out-migration of adult
males is very high, influencing the sexual division of labour for those left behind. The only means for most women to increase their yields is through harder
work, using more labour-intensive methods to maintain soil regeneration and
fertility. Where technical innovations such as irrigation techniques have made
more than one cropping season possible, as in many parts of the Sahel, women's
increased labour has been crucial in meeting the intensified work demands. But
women have not simply accepted increasing demands on their labour time. As
examples from rice development schemes in Gambia, Cameroon and Nigeria
have shown, women often have bargained with men to increase what they get in
exchange for the labour they expend on family fields (Manuh 1998); FAO 2005;
ILO 2003).

Special attention will also have to be paid to rural women in Sub-Saharan
Africa where development is low and the poverty rate high. The transformation
of the State's relationship to the economies of sub-Saharan African countries
and the dynamic changes in the agricultural sector over the past years have done
little in reducing poverty or improving their situation (ADC 1999). Sub-
Saharan Africa can develop only when all members of the community participate, and this will occur   only when women are the subjects rather than the ob-
jects of development. The recognition of the role women play in agriculture and
rural society is fundamental to agricultural and rural development in sub-
Saharan Africa. More importantly, recognition and support of this role are crucial for the development of women and the realization of their economic potential.

ACCESS TO LAND AND OTHER PRODUCTIVE RESOURCES

Even though rrural women play a predominant role in agriculture, socio-cultural
factors inhibit their access to land a key resource in agriculture. While legal

progress has been made in the last few years, the access to and control over land are still low and limited for most rural women. It has been recorded that although women are heads of family of a fifth of rural homes, and in some regions a third of such homes, they only own approximately 1% of the land. Women are denied both ownership and effective use of such productive resources. This has intensified the difficulties and limitations to the access of credit, technical assistance and participation, all of which are essential for development. New technologies and inputs are channelled primarily towards cash crops (the domain of men) and women lack the money required to purchase inputs as well as the knowledge and skills to apply them.

The land situation of rural women and that of women in general, appear even more critical in Africa. As reported by Manu (1998), across Africa, agricultural intensification, population growth and economic change have led to substantive shifts from common property systems of tenure towards more centralized resource control. In the process, women and poorer people generally have lost out. An FAO "synthesis report" on nine countries (Benin, Burkina Faso, Congo, Mauritania, Morocco, Namibia, Sudan, Tanzania and Zimbabwe) showed that women rarely own land and when they do; their holdings tend to be smaller and less fertile than those of men. Where land reform schemes have been introduced, they have often displaced complex systems of land use and tenure in which women held certain rights in common law and local practice, if not in legislation. New land titles have usually been registered in the name of a male household head regardless of women's economic contribution to the household, their customary rights or the increasing number of female-headed households.

As a result of "women in development" policy approaches and NGO activities, some women have been granted land to start communal gardens from which they generate income. When these gardens are visibly remunerative, women's continued access to rights become vulnerable and subject to encroachment by male landowners. In some parts of northern Ghana, land that women have carefully tended has been taken away, leaving them with less fertile and more distant plots.

The low incomes and increased uncertainties and risks that women face in their production activities, compounded by the lack of access to land, are pushing many of them out of traditional agriculture and into petty trading. A guaranteed right of access to land, credit and new and appropriate technology drives progress and opens the way to increased productivity and sustainable agricultural development.

EDUCATION

Education is a fundamental right for all citizens. It constitutes an essential tool to develop critical interest among people and improves their capacity for decision making on a more solid basis. With education, people will have a better knowledge of their rights, better negotiation skills and they will succeed in making their interests known and working to obtain advances in the rural world. Globally, women represent 2/3 of the illiterate population, receive less education than men and constitute the majority of the illiterate population. Their vocational and technical training is even more neglected than their general education, and agricultural extension service is primarily directed towards men. The situation is even worse in Sub-Saharan Africa. Women constitute the majority of the poor and the illiterate in both urban and rural areas in Africa. Female illiteracy rates are over 60% compared to 41% for men. Certain countries have extremely high rates: Burkina Faso at 91.1%, Sierra Leone at 88.7%, Chad at 82.1% and Guinea at 86.6% (Manu 1998). Current statistics may show slight improvement. Generally, literacy classes for women appear to have limited impact, though programmes linked to income generating activities have been relatively successful. Illiteracy, as well as capital and legal constraints, limits women's access to modern markets. Women need to acquire skills in health, technology, marketing, accounting and business management.

Women and girls are subject to food discrimination and damaging cultural practices such as genital mutilation, and they lack information on nutrition and health. Globalization and structural adjustment policies have brought unemployment and undermined social services. Conscious effort to educate rural women on their rights and opportunities could help them overcome the negative impact of these policies. To take advantage of social services, training and other opportunities, women need to be informed of their rights and organize as a group. Information and education to promote changes in social and cultural behaviour are crucial to help overcome rural-based problems (UNESCO 2001).

CONCLUSION

In addition to experiencing most of the agonies of all women, rural women are faced with several other inhibiting factors which affect their productivity and development. This chapter has shown that rural women contribute massively to rural labor, income generation, agriculture, and household management. Meanwhile, they suffer so much marginalization, poverty, illiteracy and limited access to productive resources. This calls for measures to improve the status of rural women which is addressed in the next chapter.

3
EFFORTS AT IMPROVING THE SITUATION OF RURAL WOMEN

INTRODUCTION

The situation of rural women has been an issue of concern to the international community for decades. The World Conferences on Women, as well as the twenty-third special session of the General Assembly in 2000 explicitly considered this issue and adopted comprehensive sets of policy recommendations as part of their outcome documents. Issues covered by these recommendations included rural women's access to and control over productive resources such as land; capital; credit and technology; questions of gainful employment and unpaid labour; participation in decision-making; food security issues and the education and health of rural women. Since 1985, the General Assembly has regularly considered the situation of rural women and adopted resolutions thereon. Recent discussions focused on the situation of rural women in the context of emerging global trends and the impact of these trends on rural development. The gender perspectives of issues such as liberalization of trade; markets for food and other agricultural products; the commercialization and modernization of agriculture and the increasing privatization of resources and services received all attention and comprehensive recommendations were proposed to improve the situation of rural women within the context of globalization.

In the follow-up to the Fourth World Conference on Women, rather than focusing specifically on the situation of rural women, the Commission on the Status of Women considered their situation as a cross-cutting concern within the framework of its deliberations on particular themes. For example, the issues of land ownership and access to other productive resources including water were discussed during the fortieth, forty- first and forty-sixth sessions when the Commission considered themes related to the Platform for Action as critical areas of concern on women and poverty and women and the environment. The

Convention on the Elimination of all Forms of Discrimination against Women (CEDAW) is unique among international human rights instruments in addressing the situation of rural women. According to article 14, "States parties shall take into account the particular problems faced by rural women and the significant roles which rural women play in the economic survival of their families, including their work in the non- monetized sectors of the economy, and shall take all appropriate measures to ensure the application of the provisions of the Convention to women in rural areas". The Convention enumerates a range of measures State's parties are expected to take to ensure that rural women can, on a basis of equality with men, participate in and benefit from rural development.

The previous chapter helped to define and analyse the situation of rural women. The analyses revealed that rural women make tremendous contribution to development and most especially management of the household. Meanwhile, because their location in rural communities makes them difficult to reach, they appear *invisible*. A review of reports of multilateral and bilateral organizations and other literature shows that efforts are being made to give focus to rural women and harness their potential for development in rural communities and society in general. This chapter explores and discusses ongoing efforts to support and build the capacity of rural women for development.

THE UNITED NATIONS' AGENDAS FOR RURAL WOMEN

The United Nations has given recognition to the role of rural women and the invisibility, disadvantages and challenges they face. At the 99th plenary meeting on the improvement of the situation of women in rural areas, several observations were made. It was noted that there was a growing awareness of Governments regarding the need for strategies and programs to improve the situation of women in rural areas. It was also observed that economic and financial crisis in many developing countries have severely affected the socio-economic status of women, especially in rural areas, and that the number of rural women living in poverty was continuing to rise. These realities called for the urgent need to take appropriate measures to further improve   the situation.

Member States were entreated to attach greater importance to the improvement of the situation of rural women when designing and developing national development strategies and to and to pay special attention to their practical and their strategic needs. This could be achieved by integrating the concerns of rural women into national development policies and programmers and placing a higher priority on budgetary allocation related to the interests of rural women. Other resolutions included:

- Strengthening national machineries and establishing institutional linkages among governmental bodies in various sectors and non-governmental organizations that are concerned with rural development
- Increasing the participation of rural women in the decision-making process

- Undertaking necessary measures to give rural women full and equal access to productive resources including the right to inheritance and to ownership of land and other property; credit/capital; natural resources; appropriate technologies; markets and information and meeting their basic requirements in water and sanitation
- Investing in the human resources of rural women, particularly through health and literacy programmers and social support measures
- The World Food Summit to be convened by the FAO of the United Nations in 1996 to give due consideration to the issue of improving the situation of rural women, taking into account their role in food production and food security. The United Nations Conference on Human Settlements (Habitat II) was also tasked to give due consideration to the gender aspects of rural-urban migration and its impact on the situation of rural women, in formulating relevant strategies and actions. (UN 1995; UN 2005a; UN 2005b)

Another resolution on rural women followed the 1995 resolution. To improve the situation of women in rural areas among all member states, the 88th Plenary Meeting of the UN in 2001outlined the following measures:

- Create an enabling environment for improving the situation of rural women
- Design and revise laws to ensure [that] where private ownership of land and property exists, rural women are accorded full and equal rights to own land and other property, including the right to inheritance
- Undertake administrative reforms and other necessary measures to give women the same right as men to credit, capital, appropriate technologies and access to markets and information
- Take steps towards ensuring that women's unpaid work and contributions to on-farm and off-farm production, including income generated in the informal sector, are visible
- Assess the feasibility of developing and improving mechanisms, such as time-use studies, to measure in quantitative terms unpaid work, recognizing the potential for it to be reflected in the formulation and implementation of policies and programmers at the national and regional levels
- Invest in and strengthen efforts to meet the basic needs of rural women through capacity-building and human resources development measures
- Provide safe and reliable water supply and health services including family planning services, and nutritional programs as well as education and literacy programs and social support measures
- Pursue the political and socio-economic empowerment of rural women by supporting their full and equal participation in decision-making at all levels, including in rural institutions through the provision of training and capacity-building programs and legal literacy

- Promote programs to enable rural women and men to reconcile their work and family responsibilities and to encourage men to share equally with women, household and childcare responsibilities
- Develop specific assistance programs and advisory services to promote economic skills of rural women in banking, modern trading and financial procedures
- Provide micro-credit and other financial and business services to a greater number of women in rural areas for their economic empowerment

The Commission on the Status of Women was also urged to pay appropriate attention to the situation of rural women in the consideration of the priority themes identified in its multi-year program of work for the period 2002-2006. The need to identify the best practices for ensuring that rural women have access to and full participation in the areas of information and communications technologies through specific studies was also emphasized. To achieve this, the International Telecommunication Union was called on to consider this matter in connection with the preparations for the World Summit on the Information Society (UN 1995; UN 2005a; UN 2005b).

These observations and resolutions indicated that, as far back as 1979, the United Nations had given recognition to the invisibility and plight of rural women and outlined strategies for improving their situation. A study of the context of the resolution (and the resolution itself) indicates that initial efforts bordered on issues that are still facing rural women of today; poor national budgetary allocations; high poverty levels among rural women; domination in the agriculture sector; effects of rural-urban migration and the need for capacity building. If these issues are still being highlighted for action, then one cannot help but question the level of commitment and extent of achievement of such interventions at both the local and international levels. Nevertheless, it is remarkable to find that International bodies have given recognition to the situation of rural women and have outlined strategies to address the issue.

CELEBRATION OF THE WORLD RURAL WOMEN'S DAY

In recognition of the contribution to development and the plight and invisibility of rural women, a day has been set for the celebration of rural women. This celebration was launched at the fourth United Nations Conference on Women in Beijing, China in 1995 by Non-Government Organizations (NGOs) which selected October 15 as the date. The Day is to be celebrated to provide rural women and their organizations with a focal point to:

- Raise the profile of rural women
- Sensitize both government and public to their crucial, yet largely unrecognized roles

- Promote action in their support
- Obtain recognition and support for the multiple roles of rural women, who are mostly farmers and small entrepreneurs
- Fight inequalities and prejudices against rural women (FAO 2005)

The theme for the Celebration for the year 2005, *Rights for Women as Rural Citizen,* highlighted the defence of the rights of rural women and the struggle against the violence suffered by the citizens of the rural world and its vital importance among the highlighted actions to be taken towards achieving the theme was to raise awareness of the contribution rural women make to small towns, communities and agriculture. It was recognized that there is the need for policies that attract women and young girls to remain in the countryside since policies which lead to an exodus of their rural communities will eventually result in a total abandonment of rural areas. To achieve the theme for the celebration, the IFAP Standing Committee on Women Farmers recommended that the attention of governments and international authorities be focussed on the following areas for action.

THE RIGHTS OF INDIGENOUS WOMEN

In recognition that indigenous women have an important role, not only in farming, but also as holders and transmitters of cultural elements that include nature as part of a global universe and the discrimination and exclusion that they suffer and the consequences of harmful traditional practices the following that they bear it was recommended that their identity should be projected, diversity was to be promoted and that plans and programs in research centres focus on strengthening the dignity of indigenous women.

THE RIGHT OF ACCESS TO NATURAL RESOURCES

In view of the fact that guaranteed right of access to land and other productive resources opens the way to increased productivity and sustainable agricultural development, the following have been proposed to help women to access natural resources:

- Obtain from political authorities a national and international commitment for an equitable and sustainable distribution of natural resources taking the local social, economical, cultural and environmental context into account
- Recognise the right of property for the women farmers as well as their right of inheritance
- ensure the taking into account of rural women on world platforms regarding a secure and sustainable right to existing natural resources

- Facilitate the access to knowledge, training and general and technical information concerning the access and management of natural resources for women farmers

LABOUR RIGHTS IN THE AGRICULTURAL SECTOR

In the agricultural sector, the overexploitation of women's labour traditionally results in an inequality of the salaries for equivalent work and competence. In many cases rural women do not benefit from a social security system since they are classed as farmers' wives. In spite of the noticeable increase of the participation of women in the world of labour in the past few years, this difference in the recognition of labour in the farming sector still persists. To obtain and adhere to labour rights in agriculture for rural women, these recommendations have been made to:

- Ensure the existence of a legislation that recognises the professional status of women farmers and the equality between men and women in the farming sector
- Take all necessary and appropriate measures in order that women farmers have full knowledge of the legislation
- Facilitate the access to knowledge and to general information about labour rights for women farmers

THE RIGHT OF RURAL WOMEN TO PARTICIPATE IN MARKETS

Trade is seen as one of the tools that could be used to ensure sustainable development worldwide. Women in general and women farmers in particular should be able to use this tool to its full extent. This will be supported by:

- Organising workshops with the aim of improving the productivity and competitiveness of women farmers
- Analysing the marketing process for the productions of rural women in order to improve its efficiency
- Training in order to improve marketing and market access in the national, regional and international markets

THE RIGHT OF WOMEN TO PARTICIPATE IN FARMERS' ORGANISATIONS AND DECISION MAKING

Priority of the interests and needs of women farmers in development policies must be taken into consideration. It is indispensable that rural women understand the details of the policies that govern them and become involved in the elaboration of the political positions of the agricultural organisations which represent them. Thus it becomes crucial to:

- Strengthen their capacities through a full and active participation in farmers' organisations and in decision making bodies
- Obtain seats for women on all the committees and working groups of farmers' organisations
- Organise and promote women's structures in farmers' organisations
- Actively participate in debates and national and international programs within the organisations and with other organisations
- Make contact with government officials in order to explain the concerns of rural women

THE RIGHT TO EDUCATION

Education is a fundamental right for all citizens and constitutes an essential tool to develop critical interest among people and improves their capacity for decision making on a more solid basis. With education, people will have a better knowledge of their rights and better negotiation skills and become more successful in making their interests known and in working to obtain advances in the rural world. Globally, women represent 2/3 of the illiterate population. To ensure the right of rural women to education, the following proposals were recommended:

- Training for women within organisations be organized with the support of development agencies
- Solid and regularly updated training be given so that rural women can defend their interests in work meetings and before the authorities
- Agricultural research and education structures be worked with in order to organise training workshops
- Knowledge be spread among rural women which can be transmitted from generation-to- generation

THE RIGHT TO HEALTH CARE

Good health is essential in achieving good results in the workplace. In order to prevent health problems in rural communities, it is necessary to improve sanitary conditions. Easier access to and better quality of health services will, among other benefits, help reduce illness in families, support women during and after pregnancy, control their fertility and improve their quality of life in both rural and urban communities. To improve the health situation and promote the health rights of women, the following recommendations have been made:

- Facilitate the access to knowledge for rural women as well as general information about health, nutrition, and child care
- Put pressure on governments through their health departments in order that these needs that have been repeatedly demonstrated in studies and field work regarding rural communities become essential premises of law
- Promote awareness campaigns about the importance of health for rural women

RIGHTS CONCERNING VIOLENCE AGAINST RURAL WOMEN

Domestic violence is a reality in rural areas. Educative work within the family unit becomes crucial to eradicate this unacceptable situation. To ensure that their rights are respected, women need access to law courts. Meanwhile, there are innumerable obstacles impeding access to justice, especially for those women who live in remote rural areas. There is absence of authorities in charge of enforcing laws as well as poor training of the existing authorities, limited access to health and law services and precariousness in the provision of services. It was therefore recommended that:

- Innovative strategies be designed to avoid violence and ways to integrate the situation into health services in collaboration with the different countries' authorities
- Awareness be raised within the population about the magnitude and extent of violence against women
- Efficient local bodies be created in rural communities that take charge of women when their rights are violated
- Awareness be raised regarding the conventions and other legal instruments that concern women's rights

WOMEN'S RIGHTS IN ARMED CONFLICTS

Conflicts and wars have tremendous effect on rural women. About 90% of the victims of today's wars are civilians, most of them women and children. In many countries, women suffer from systematic raping used as a war tactic. Other forms of violence include assassinations, sexual slavery, forced pregnancy, compulsory sterilisation and recruiting of women as combatants. The Committee made the following recommendations for addressing the situation of rural women and conflicts:

- Call for legislative reforms in cases of conflict with effective supervision in order to enforce the respect of women

- Facilitate the access to public services, education, health care, police protection, telephone and transportation services in order to avoid violence against women in cases of conflict
- Activate existing measures to accelerate the protection of women's rights in cases of conflict
- Promote an equitable participation of women in the solution of conflicts

This comprehensive range of recommendations from agricultural, education and health through   conflict resolution could help the advancement of and the adherence to the legal rights of rural women, if supported by commitment and effective implementation. The document which outlines the recommendations admits that the Beijing platform, adopted 10 years ago by the United Nations, was a great step forward and has produced noticeable achievements. However, there remains a long way to go to obtain these rights. Many obstacles must still be overcome if women are to fully make their voices increasingly heard in the world. This calls for a high level of commitment and hard work if we are to achieve the outlined recommendations. The surprising thing is that there are no timelines for achieving the recommendations by which one can track and assess progress.

ADULT EDUCATIONAL AND TRAINING EFFORTS

It has been acknowledged that human capital is a unique and pivotal factor in development. It is both an active agent of change and a beneficiary of change and progress. When its potentials are developed, human capital is the only one that can create, modify, apply and utilize the other capitals such as technological and natural resources for sustainable development. As human capital, rural women in developing and other countries present many relevant issues, some of which include their large numbers and their relatively low economic value. Hence, their capacity needs to be developed to enhance their capabilities. There are cases which demonstrate how training and educational activities have helped to improve the situation and capabilities of rural women. For example, Chinese women reported in China Daily, 2003.

The impact of this training shows the urgent need to take a variety measures in order to tap the potential of rural women who are plagued by outdated concepts and lack both information and technology. Getting them to recognize the principle of gender equality might be the first step in the education program. When rural women realize their value, they will be able to tap their potential. For a long time, rural women have been satisfied with being housewives, believing that their only responsibility is to care for their family and that only men are capable of earning money.

Box 1 – Case of Training Programme for Rural Women in China

Awakening Rural Women's Potential

Recognising that most poverty-stricken rural women were engaged in backward production due to a lack of educational and training opportunities, an educational programme was organised for some rural women in China by the Rural Women Magazine. The education program sponsored by the magazine aimed to assist rural women to develop themselves through enhancing their self-confidence and providing them with information and technology. Some of the beneficiaries testified that the attendance of the first symposium on rural women's development and policies held by Rural Women magazine was a turning point in their life. It gave opportunity for the women to meet many activists from women's organizations as well as making sincere friends at the symposium. It is reported by the China Daily that the programme challenged the women's outdated concepts, broadened their horizons and strengthened their confidence. As an impact, most women have changed from being rural housewives to village leadership, fighting against poverty for prosperity. One remarkable activity that has emerged from this is leading 40 rural women in building the ecological park. With the training support, rural women are playing increased significant role in the country's agriculture.

Testimonies of some of the women included the following:

- *My success proves that women can also do what men can do although we may suffer more hardships than men.*
- *After the classes, I realized that I could not stay at home and complain about my situation, my husband and society. I gained enough confidence, improved my outlook and changed my life.*

The report adds that as a result of the training, one woman began to plant fruits with advanced technology. After a few years of hard work, she has achieved goals she had previously not even dared to imagine - joining the Communist Party of China and earning 10,000 Yuan (US$1,200) a year.

(China Daily January 30, 2003); (Yuan 2003)

Numerous rural women (just as talented and hard-working as these Chinese women) will need interventions if they are to break free. Rural Women's aid and education programs that teach self-respect, self-confidence and independence are mainly organized by women's federations... Unfortunately, due to a lack of practical work, follow-ups and adequate material support, most of the training remains an empty slogan and much work remains to be done in this respect. The potential of rural women is still yet to be fully tapped. *Indeed, rural women are like a precious underground resource;* once this resource it is explored, the energy released will be massive, pushing country's economy further forward.

AN AFRICAN EFFORT

Women provide the backbone of the rural economy in much of sub-Saharan Africa. About 80% of the economically active female labour force is employed in agriculture and women comprise about 47% of the total agricultural labour force. Food production is the major activity of rural women and their responsibilities and labour inputs often exceed those of men in most areas in Africa. Women also provide much of the labour for men's cultivation of export crops; labour from which women derive little direct benefit. In 1996, in a survey of nine African countries, the UN Food and Agriculture Organization (FAO) found that women's contribution to the production of food crops ranges from 30% in Sudan to 80% in the Republic of Congo, with estimates for other countries tending toward the higher end of the scale. Women are responsible for 70% of food production: 50% of domestic food storage; 100% of food processing; 50% of animal husbandry and 60% of agricultural marketing. This indicates the need to target and support them for rural development in Africa. The West African Rural Development Centre (WARD) located in The Gambia is the intervention for improving the situation of rural women in Africa. The Centre's purpose is to improve the quality of life of West African rural people on a sustainable basis, according to their needs, through training and education to meet priority needs in the area of rural community development.

Most of the people living in the West African countries of The Gambia, Sierra Leone, Liberia, Ghana, Nigeria, Niger, Burkina Faso, Mali, Senegal, Guinea-Bissau, Guinea, Benin, Togo, Mauritania, Cameroon, Cape Verde and Côte d'Ivoire are among the poorest in the world. The education and training of rural adults, especially women, are critical to their countries' growth and development. The conditions in the countries speak eloquently to the need for rural community development training in the West African region. These West African countries share similar social conditions which include spiralling inflation; economic stagnation; environmental degradation; enormous health problems and a shift of rural inhabitants to urban areas which is creating shanty towns and exacerbating tensions in the cities. In Ghana, for example, where there were only 8 urban centres in 1900, there are now 180. If this trend continues, it is estimated that over half of the Ghanaian population will live in urban centres by 2020. Other problems aggravating the situation are civil wars and social disturbances which have destroyed much of the educational and community development infrastructure in Sierra Leone and Liberia, and crippled aid agencies operating in Nigeria. All of these West African countries are attempting to address the problems detailed above. One of the key strategies adopted has been to strengthen the rural sector. The development literature, whether from the World Bank or *The New Internationalist*, have been clear on at least one point: the key to everything from sustainable economic development to population control, is the education of women. Two major barriers affecting rural women's participation in adult education activities include the concentration of programs in urban areas and the relative lack of training of those educators and community workers operating in rural areas. The West African countries are making an effort to address this problem. In Ghana, the government implemented a program to transfer 12,000 people a year to rural areas. The Gambia created the National Vocational Training Program to provide improved rural vocational training with the objective of providing rural primary school leavers with basic skills in home economics, horticulture, literacy, trades and hygiene. These efforts have yielded some results.

As often the case in such initiatives, no provision was made for the training of facilitators. The West African nations' priorities for rural development have therefore been hampered not only by limited budgetary allocations but by a lack of trained staff that are able to deliver effective instruction and animation to adults living in rural communities. Field workers attached to aid agencies and NGO projects often require enhanced training. With the increased demand for facilitators able to operate in the areas of health care, literacy, agriculture and community development, the need for a culturally appropriate and socially relevant training and curriculum development becomes enormous.

To help support the human resource base of rural training programmes, the WARD Centre provides a database of training and curriculum development services in critical areas of community development; animator training; small/medium enterprise development; community/women's health services; literacy and project management. The objective of the WARD program is to enhance the quantity and quality of rural programs in such areas as literacy, nutrition, health education and community development and to target women at the village level (WARD 2006). The emphasis on increasing access to programs for strengthening women individually and collectively is essential for WARD. For the past seven years, WARD has worked with Gambian and Ghanaian women to identify and overcome obstacles enhance participation of women in their "triple-roles" in reproductive, productive and community management. WARD has developed materials that address the changing roles of women in rural Africa and provide' a basis for adult educators to identify with rural people the advantages, as well as the stresses, of these changes. With support from African collaborators, WARD has also created role plays (within a culturally appropriate context) which include structured activities and discussion topics that deal effectively with the issue of women in rural African society.

Women's associations and organizations have also supported the capacity building of rural women. Many rural women in Africa belong to women-only mutual-aid societies, benevolent groups in churches, cooperatives and market women's groups. Some of these groups permit women to pool resources which allow them to reduce their workload and invest in savings societies or cooperative ventures. These cooperative societies have provided women access to resources. For example, the Corn Mill societies in Cameroon, the *Six S* associations in Burkina Faso and the General Union of Cooperatives in Mozambique which supply most of Maputo's fruits and vegetables. In Benin, only 8% of rural women belong to formal cooperatives, but an estimated 90% participate in traditional women's savings and credit groups. Informal rotating credit associations in Ghana, Tanzania, Gambia and Zimbabwe have been used by the estimated 25% of economically active women in the non-agricultural informal sector to invest in businesses and farms, home improvements and school costs for their children (WARD 2006).

SOME CONSIDERATIONS FOR TRAINING

Vocational and technical training has a long and rich experience of intervention worldwide. The purpose of the interventions is to support the labour integration of rural women, especially in micro-entrepreneurial activities. These interventions offer good practice and successful learning opportunities to a new generation of policies that are directed at articulating and enhancing gender mainstreaming with positive discrimination actions in order to improve and enhance rural women's personal and labour-life quality. Exploring the potential of vocational and technical training for rural women and promoting methodological innovation, entrepreneurship and training in new technologies will obviously help activate rural industries.

To enhance and ensure effectiveness of rural training programmes, gender perspectives will have to be incorporated in training policies. Taking a gender perspective in all interventions helps to illuminate the nature of rural poverty. A gender perspective looks at how and why men and women experience poverty differently and become poor through different processes and, in turn, how rural development presents different opportunities and challenges for men and women. Evaluations have shown that if gender specificities are not taken into account, projects may increase women's workload, thus affecting their caregiving responsibilities and health. Projects may also negatively affect women's control over resources and technologies. Gender analysis in design and gender-sensitive monitoring and evaluation is needed to identify risks and recommend preventive measures. Approaches that have succeeded in one place may not be applicable in another. Specific mainstreaming strategies need to be developed to suit different project contexts .This approach helps the implementation of current actions of positive discrimination in order to overcome initial disadvantages women may have at the outset and seeks to promote training for technologically innovating areas, and participation in development organizations etc.

FOCUS ON RURAL YOUTH

The case of rural youth is also crucial for rural development. The positive impact programs targeting young rural women, their families and communities could make on their personal and rural development is of much importance. Both rural young women and men are often neglected due to the overwhelming concern for immediate solutions to national problems, especially in urban areas. There is also the perception that youth are not yet productive and contributing members of society. Recognising this, recommendations were made at an FAO Expert Consultative meeting that FAO intensify its advocacy efforts on behalf of rural youth, by playing a larger role in assisting governments in formulating national youth policies and developing action programmes for creating and/or strengthening youth programs (FAO 1996).

CONCLUSION

The situation of rural women is determined by their multiple responsibilities for the care and well-being of their families and the community, household tasks and farm and non-farm income-generating activities. Although often unrecognized, women play a focal role in the survival strategies and economy of poor rural households across all geographical regions. Increasing the economic resilience of the poor is largely about enabling women to realize their socioeconomic potential more fully and improve the quality of their lives. Thus, women need access to productive natural resources, services, knowledge and technologies, and must be active in decision-making processes.

It appears that much has been done to improve the situation of rural women in terms of passing resolutions for international commitment, interventions and support; celebration of a Rural Women's World Day and undertaking capacity building programmes. The potential of innovative information and communication technology and recognition of gender dimensions in all interventions has also been explored. The need to focus on rural youth has also been highlighted. The task for change and development agents is to find ways to stay committed to the agenda for improving the situation of rural women. Rural women cannot wait any longer. The development of rural communities and nations requires their full participation and will happen only when women of all categories, most especially those in rural communities, are perceived and treated as subjects and not objects of development.

4
ADULT EDUCATION FOR DEVELOPMENT – INTERNATIONAL PERSPECTIVES

INTRODUCTION

From the Universal Declaration of Human Rights in 1948 through the Declaration of the International Conference on Adult Education (ICAE) in Hamburg in 1997, to the World Forum on Education for All in Dakar in 2000, an international consensus has been reached on the right to education and the right to learn throughout life for women and men. There has also been a consensus on the central role of adult education in support of creative and democratic citizenship. As the Hamburg (1997) the Declaration stated: "The informed and effective participation of men and women in every sphere of life is needed if humanity is to survive and meet the challenges of the future". Adult education promotes life-long learning as a necessary component for people to contribute creatively if people are creatively contribute to their communities and live in independent, democratic societies. Adult and lifelong learning is linked to social; economic and political justice; equality of gender relations; the universal right to learn; living in harmony with the environment; respect for human rights; recognition of cultural diversity; promotion of peace and the active involvement of women and men in decisions affecting their lives. Adult education has tremendous potential for development of the human resources and society at large. It is in this regard that this chapter (and indeed this book) explores the potential of adult education for improving the lot of women and society at large towards poverty reduction. This chapter reviews the International Conference of Adult Education (ICAE, 2004) which focused on poverty reduction.

WHAT IS ADULT EDUCATION?

Adult education is complex in nature, multi-focused and multi-dimensional. As a result of its multi-focused nature, defining adult education becomes a complex task. It is difficult to comprehend the concept, especially in communities where there are *misleading* adult educational programmes in which adult education comprises a wide range of educational programs in which adults participate. The key word in the definition of adult education is *adult*. If an individual, who is accepted as an adult by the society in which the person belongs, is engaged in any form of educational program, that engagement could be labelled as *adult education*. The type, content or goal of the educational programme does not matter much. Different adults have different educational needs. For adults who have never had formal education their educational need could be basic literacy (reading, writing and numeracy). For others it is the education of their culture; skill training; computer literacy; education on current issues; political education; commerce; career enhancement or degree programmes. In order to target and engage the adults in an educational program or activity that will be of immediate relevance to them, organising adult educational programs often begins with a needs assessment and to help identify what adults want to learn and what they perceive to be their educational gaps and needs(Knowles, M, 1990). Thus, in the professional or ideal sense, adult educational programmes become more de-mand-driven than supply-driven. *The learners determine what they want to learn.*

There have been several definitions of adult education. A study of some of them will broaden our understanding of the adult education concept. Correlative to the definition of adult education provided in the 1976 UNESCO Recommen-dation on the Development of Adult Education, the Hamburg Declaration of 1997 emphasised the following: "Adult education denote (sic) the entire body of ongoing learning processes, formal or otherwise, whereby people regarded as adults by the society to which they belong develop their abilities, enrich their knowledge, and improve their technical or professional qualifications or turn them in a new direction to meet their own needs and those of their society."

The Encarta Reference Library (2005) gives a brief definition of adult edu-cation as: "All forms of schooling and learning programs in which adults par-ticipate."

Thus, adult learning thus encompasses formal and continuing education, non-formal learning and the spectrum of informal and incidental learning avail-able in a multicultural learning society, where theoretical and practice-based approaches are recognized.

Adult educational programmes vary in organization from casual, incidental learning to formal college credit courses. These include non-formal educational programmes; formal educational programs like university credit courses; liter-acy training; community development; on-the-job training and continuing pro-fessional education. Such a wide spectrum of education is provided by a variety of institutions such as colleges; libraries; museums; social services; government agencies; businesses; non-governmental organizations and Churches.

A person's desire to participate in an educational program is often the result of a changing personal, social or vocational situation. This individual orientation has resulted in the creation of a continually changing, dynamic field, able to respond to the varied needs of society. Recognizing the need to update information and skills for development, the desire for knowledge and information is also increasing among women. Rapidly changing technical fields also require constant updating of information in order for workers to remain effective and productive.

Another major development in Adult Education is in the delivery system. Radio, network television, cable television, internet and other electronic media are increasingly being used for adult education. Broadcast media are being used worldwide to provide public information, teach reading and writing, conduct specialized seminars and short courses and provide university-degree programs. These electronic media offer the means for reaching homebound populations and geographically isolated rural communities.

BEGINNINGS OF ADULT EDUCATION

As an educational practice or process, adult education is as old as the first adults that walked the surface of the earth. Though it is still in the continuing process of developing as a discipline and a profession, early formal adult education activities focused on single needs such as reading and writing. Originally, many early programs were started by Churches to teach people to read the Bible. When the original purpose was satisfied, programs were often adjusted to meet more general educational needs of the population. When libraries, lecture series and discussion societies began in various countries during the 18th Century, more people experienced the benefits of education and began to increasingly participate in social, political, and occupational activities. By the 19th century, adult education was developing as a formal, organized movement in the Western and developing worlds.

Encarta (2005) explains that adult education has long been important in Europe and other parts of the world, where formal educational programs began in the 18th century. For example, the Danish folk high school movement in the mid-19th century prevented the loss of the Danish language and culture which a strong German influence was threatening to absorb. In Britain, concern for the education of the poor and working-class people resulted in the growth of adult education programs i.e., the evening school and the Mechanic's Institute to expand educational opportunities for all people. After the Russian Revolution, the Soviet government virtually eliminated illiteracy through the establishment of various institutions and extension classes for adults. In other parts of the world, adult education movements are of a more recent origin. In 1960 Egypt established *schools for the people* system designed to educate the adult population. In the 1970s, after many years in which the primary educational concern was with creating public school systems for children, countries in Africa, Asia, and Latin America began to increase opportunities for adult education. Innovative programs involving the mass media are now being used in many countries. For example, Tanzania has used mass-education techniques and radio to organize national education programs in health, nutrition and citizenship.

As it happened in other parts of the world in the 1940s, adult education in West Africa served as a tool for cultural transmission. To equip them for European culture, illiterate adults were the taught literacy skills of reading and writing, while the literates were *enhanced* in literacy and liberal education to transform them into *ladies* and *gentlemen*. In the 1950s, political and nationalistic dimensions were added to adult educational activities. Using the print medium, nationalists of West Africa educated their followers in the struggle for self-government. Instead of a systematized, formal adult education process, mass political education was promoted. Economic and functional education was not predominant. Following the attainment of independence by some of the West African nations, there was increased drive for adult education. Political education increased in countries like Ghana, Guinea and Mali. Ruling political parties used adult educational associations to promote their political manifestoes as national ideologies and overshadowed the promotion of adult education as a functional instrument for socio-economic development (Akinpelu, 1979).

In Ghana, Amedzro (2004) explains that as a result of the limited educational opportunities in the formal school system, voluntary adult education associations emerged as far back as the 1830s. These associations engaged in discussions to keep abreast of the times and improve upon their educational standards and provided literacy programmes for illiterates. Some wanted further studies for promotion and salary increment. Through this process, adult education in Ghana has progressed to the university level to provide both formal and non-formal education to the masses.

The Non-Formal Education Division (NFED) is the government machinery used for delivering basic adult basic literacy in Ghana. Launched in 1991, in an effort to facilitate rural and national development, the National Functional Literacy Program has undertaken several activities to accelerate reduction of illiteracy in the country. An NFED report on the celebration of the International Literacy Day (2005) specifies that the National Functional Literacy Program provides reading, writing, numeracy and an enabling environment for learners to acquire income-generating skills in income generation project classes. Leaders of these projects are trained in entrepreneurship; management; book keeping; fund sourcing and marketing skills. However, beneficiaries are trained in skills like cassava processing; kente (a local, royal cloth) weaving; batik and tie-dye making; beekeeping and baking. An English literacy programme was established to expand the learning scope of learners to strengthen their public communication skills. Over the period of operation, the NFED's achievements include an annual average intake of 200,000 learners with a total recruitment of 2,505,709 and a total of 1,669,210 graduates of the programme. Its community development achievements include provision of potable water, child day care centres, classrooms and market sheds. Some learners have graduated into the formal educational system to the tertiary level while others have taken responsible roles in the communities to serve as Traditional Birth Attendants, religious leaders, District Assembly persons and Unit Committee chairpersons (NFED 2005).

This background information shows how adult education has been used as a tool for cultural transmission, skill building, citizenship or political education and enhancement of individual capabilities for national development at the international, West African and Ghanaian scenes. Though history reveals that some political agencies have used adult education to promote their political agendas, continuous creation of educational opportunities for all adults could no doubt equip the current generation for nation building. A literate population is a necessity for any nation wishing to take advantage of modern technological growth. Research has shown a direct relationship between literacy among women and improved health and child care in the family indicating that adult educational activities which target women could lead to their empowerment. Among current developments in Adult Education is its use for poverty reduction. Adult educators are caught in a dilemma between the possibilities of a genuinely democratic and sustainable learning society and the passivity, poverty, vulnerability and chaos that economic globalization is creating everywhere. This calls for the commitment to work for an equitable world where all forms of discrimination are eliminated and peace and development are possible. The latest International Conference of Adult Education (ICAE, 2004) therefore focused on the use of adult education for poverty reduction among all, including women.

BROADENING THE SCOPE AND RE-CONSOLIDATING ADULT EDUCATION AND FOCUSING ON INTERNATIONAL CONFERENCES OF ADULT EDUCATION

In response to current trends, adult education has gone through a series of developments leading towards reviewing and expanding its scope. One development initiative is the 1976 UNESCO Recommendation on the Development of Adult Education which set forth the vital role of adult education *as forming part of lifelong education and learning*. The recommendation focused on content and management issues of Adult Education and its recommendation focussed on definition; aim; content in youth and adult education; adult education and work; building the capacity of adult educators; methods; research; evaluation; structures; management and administration, and international cooperation in Adult Education. The following review of the *Hamburg Declaration* and *Agenda for the Future* that emerged from the 1997 Conference, the 2004 Conference that followed and other initiatives highlights the evolving focus of adult education.

THE 1997 INTERNATIONAL CONFERENCE
OF ADULT EDUCATION AND BEYOND

The CONFINTEA V Conference in Hamburg reaffirmed that it is only in human-centred development in a participatory society based on the full respect of human rights that will lead to sustainable and equitable development. The representatives of governments and organizations that participated in the CONFINTEA V explored the potential and the future of adult learning, broadly and dynamically conceived within a framework of lifelong learning as these were outlined in detail in the *Agenda for the Future* and the *Conference Declaration*.

Taking into consideration current international and societal developments, the *Agenda for the Future* focused on the new commitment to the development of adult learning. The Agenda targeted common concerns facing humanity on the eve of the 21st Century and the vital role that adult learning must play in enabling women and men of all ages to face these urgent challenges with knowledge, courage and creativity. The Agenda acknowledges that profound changes are taking place both globally and locally as evidenced in a globalization of economic systems, the rapid development of science and technology, the age structure and mobility of populations, and the emergence of an information and knowledge-based society. The world is also experiencing major changes in patterns of work and unemployment, a growing ecological crisis, and tensions between social groups based on culture, ethnicity, gender roles, religion and income. These trends call for the enforcement and provision of Adult Education in an innovative way.

Similarly, the International Commission on Education for the 21st Century observed that the concept of learning throughout life is the key that gives access to the 21st Century and goes beyond the traditional distinctions between initial and continuing education. It links up with a *new concept* of the learning society, in which everything should afford an opportunity for learning and fulfilling one's potential. The Commission's report emphasized the importance of the four pillars of education: *learning to know, learning to do, learning to live together and learning to be.*

In 1997, The Agenda for the Future of Adult Education covered a broad and complex spectrum of adult learning under ten thematic headings:

1.   Adult learning and democracy: the challenges of the twenty-first century
2.   Improving the conditions and quality of adult learning
3.   Ensuring the universal right to literacy and basic education
4.   Adult learning, gender equality and equity, and the empowerment of women
5.   Adult learning and the changing world of work

6.   Adult learning in relation to environment, health and population
7.   Adult learning, culture, media and new information technologies
8.   Adult learning for all: the rights and aspirations of different groups
9.   The economics of adult learning
10.   Enhancing international co-operation and solidarity

The key players in the process of using Adult Education for human development have been identified to include partnership between government departments; intergovernmental and non-governmental organizations; employers and trade unions; universities and research centres and the media; civil and community-level associations; facilitators of adult learning and the adult learners themselves.

The Declaration of Conference which is reflected in the Agenda for the Future sought to re-direct and re-consolidate the focus of Adult Education in the following core areas:

Basic and Youth Education: The Declaration highlighted that basic education for all is defined as people who, whatever their age, have an opportunity, individually and collectively, to realize their potential. It is not only a right but a duty and a responsibility both to others and to society. The youth must be given a second chance to education or training to acquire employable skills even after they have passed the basic school-going age or dropped out. By so doing, nations will be in good position to overcome the problem of unemployment among the youth.

This approach calls for the need to adopt innovative approaches in the educational policies of developing countries. Opportunities like the National Youth Employment Programmes in Ghana whereby the Government is providing training for the unemployed youth and thereby provided a *second-chance education* for the youth. Educational institutions and leaders of policies of education may have to review their systems and provide avenues for drop-outs to join the mainstream education at any age.

Another option is to intensify non-formal skill-building programs that will meet the learning needs of the youth who may have to combine work with studies. There are some youth who dropped out of formal education for economic reasons and therefore could only continue their studies if they have the opportunity to keep their jobs. With the emergence of new information and communication technology packages for distance learning, some youth could conveniently combine work and study from any geographical location. Providing a wide publicity of such existing programs will make it known and accessible to most youths in remote areas.

The Ageing Population: Much as Adult Educators are giving a clarion call to focus on younger adults, the aging population have also remained a crucial target group in adult educational programs and have been increasing in number over the years. These older adults have much to contribute to the development of society. It is important that they have the opportunity to learn on equal terms and in age-appropriate ways. Their skills and abilities should be recognized, valued and made use of. Adult education for the senior population will equip them with new skills even after they have retired from active service.

Adult Literacy: Literacy has been a core part of Adult Education for several years and been the focus in the world of Adult Education for so long that most people associate all forms of Adult Education, but it is much broader than that. Literacy broadly defined conceived as being *the basic knowledge and skills needed by all in a rapidly changing world, is a fundamental human right.* Everywhere in the world, literacy has become the gateway to fuller participation in social, cultural, political and economic life. Literate populations are able to make informed decisions in their various communities. The world is moving rapidly toward democracy and participation. In every country an informed population is a contributing factor to the success of democracy. As a result, Adult Educators have called for the content of literacy programs to be relevant to people's socio-economic and cultural contexts. With the relevance of such educational packages and the immediacy application to people's lives, adults who live busy lives will more readily commit to the process of learning. The principle of Adult Education advocates that the relevance of education to the occupation and daily engagements of the adults motivates them to learn. Literacy should enable individuals to function effectively in their societies and make them active citizens of their nation states. It should be a process in which communities affect their own cultural, political and social transformations and enable the citizenry to understand the interconnections between personal, local and global realities. Considering the male-female percentage in society, for a balance in knowledge and contribution to development, literacy programs must obviously focus on *both males and females and address their needs equally.*

To facilitate a lifelong learning process that will create a literate population, literacy programs have to remain a part of all educational packages. The creation of flexible learning systems and preconditions for learning through sensitization and empowerment programs would be effective. Adult educators should therefore be committed to ensuring opportunities for all people to acquire and maintain literacy skills and to creating a literate environment to preserve and support oral culture. Providing learning opportunities for all people [including the unreached and the excluded such as women, youth and rural settlers], should be a most urgent concern for all.

Culture of Peace and Education for Citizenship and Democracy: In the search for peace and democracy [which de facto create enabling environment for education and development]. Adult Educators have not overlooked this very important area. One of the foremost challenges today is the elimination of the culture of violence and the construct of a culture of peace based on justice and tolerance; a culture in which dialogue, mutual recognition and negotiation will replace violence in homes and communities: within nations and between countries. The contribution of Adult Education cannot be denied in this process. Adult educational activities for promotion of peace and democracy must concern itself with issues of conflicts, strategies for peace building and reconciliation approaches. As a strategy for faster and sustainable results, such constructs could form the content of broad or nationwide literacy programs.

Diversity and Equality: Diversity is natural and will forever be with mankind. And it has its own beauty that cannot be underrated. What is most important is the ability to promote equity in the face of diversity and concerns Adult Educators *around* the globe. They are committed to reflecting the richness of cultural diversity and respect for traditional and indigenous peoples' knowledge and systems of learning. One facilitation instrument is the respect for and promotion of the right to learn in the Mother Tongue. Intercultural education needs to be presented in such a way as to encourage learning between and about different cultures in support of peace; human rights and fundamental freedoms; democracy; justice; liberty; coexistence, and diversity. Making provision for these in adult educational activities will help to gain the full participation and commitment of indigenous peoples. In this way it will minimized dominance of populous groups, discrimination, intimidation and struggles for power.

Indigenous Education and Culture: Diversity in society leads to and calls for diversity in the delivery of education. There are diverse groups of people who need to be targeted and dealt with differently. Such group of people include indigenous peoples and nomadic peoples, both of which have the right of access to *all* levels and forms of education provided by the State, and are not to be denied the right to enjoy their own culture or to use their own languages in the process. A one-size-fit-all type of educational policies and packages may not be suitable for such people. They may require a type of education that meets their lifestyle and socio-cultural and economic needs. Special efforts are therefore required to provide access to such peoples. For this reason, Adult Educators have declared that education for indigenous and nomadic peoples should be linguistically and culturally appropriate to their needs and should facilitate access to further education and training.

Health: Public Health Education is a critical element in all adult educational programs Health, education and development cannot be separated. Similarly, to education, *health is a basic human right*. The two are not separable. Adult Educators have declared that investments in education are indeed investments in health. Lifelong learning that includes health education can contribute substantially to the promotion of health and the prevention of diseases. It is therefore the responsibility of adult educators to offer significant opportunities for these people to receive relevant, equitable and sustainable access to health knowledge.

Environmental Sustainability: The sustenance of mankind depends on the sustenance of the environment. If Adult Educators want to have a sustained community of people then they cannot overlook environmental issues. With education as their weapon, Adult Educations advocate for a lifelong learning process of education for environmental sustainability which recognizes that ecological problems exist within a socio-economic, political and cultural context. Thus a sustainable future cannot be achieved without addressing the relationship between environmental problems and current development paradigms. Adult environmental education programmers have therefore been called to make it their business and play a significant role in sensitizing and mobilizing communities and decision-makers toward sustained environmental action.

Transformation of the Economy: The power of a sound economy cannot be underrated. Nation States are seeking economic growth that provides a safety net for their growing population. *One cannot study on an empty stomach.* Globalization, changes in production patterns, rising unemployment and the difficulty of ensuring secure livelihoods call for more active labour policies and increased investments in developing the necessary skills which will enable men and women to participate in the labor market and in income-generating activities. Promotion of continuous education that equips the adult population for increased productivity and keeps them informed to effectively participate and compete in the labor market becomes crucial.

Access to Information: Much as ICTs have tremendous potential of serving as an instrument for packaging and delivering education to all corners of the globe and promoting development, they can also create divides in society if not utilised appropriately and responsibly. The development of the new ICTs brings with it new risks of social and occupational exclusion for groups of individuals and even businesses which refuse, resist or are unable to adapt to the ICT context. Conscious effort is required to harness the potential of ICTs. Basic ICT facilities like radio have been very useful for making adult educational programs accessible to people in the remotest parts of every region. One of the roles of adult education should therefore be to limit the risks of exclusion of ICT user facilities so that the Information Society is created in every village of the globe.

Women's Integration and Empowerment: Targeting women for holistic development has featured prominently on the platforms of Adult *Education*. Being an educational system that sets the target to develop the potential of the marginalized in society, Adult Education has given great prominence to the important issue of women's empowerment. Conference recognized that women have a right to equal opportunities. To enable women of all ages to make their full contribution to society and to the resolution of the multiple problems confronting humanity, equal opportunity in all aspects of education is essential. When women are found in a situation of social isolation and lack access to knowledge and information, they are alienated from decision-making processes within the family, community and society in general, and have little control over their bodies and lives. *For poor women, the struggle for survival becomes an obstacle to education even as society continues to depend on their full contribution in all fields of work and aspects of life.*

Considering the priority that female education deserves and requires, Adult Educators have strongly insisted that any attempts to restrict women's right to literacy, education and training must be considered unacceptable. And where they do exist, practices and measures should be taken to counter them. Educational processes should address the constraints that prevent women's access to intellectual resources and empower women to become fully active as partners in social transformation. In this process, the message of equality and equal access must not be limited to programs intended for women only. In order to change this situation and build their capacity to gain access to formal power structures and decision-making processes in both private and public spheres, adult educators should, as an empowering strategy, ensure that women are made aware of the need to organize as a group.

Some of the specific strategies that have been outlined in the *Agenda for the Future* for the promotion of empowerment of women and gender equity through adult learning include:

- Recognizing and correcting the continued marginalization and denial of access and of equal opportunities for quality education
- Ensuring that all women and men are provided with the necessary education to meet their basic needs and to exercise their human rights
- Combating domestic and sexual violence by providing appropriate education for men and supplying information and counselling to increase women's ability to protect themselves from such violence
- Removing barriers to access to formal and non-formal education in the case of pregnant adolescents and young mothers
- Promoting a gender-sensitive participatory pedagogy which acknowledges the daily life experience of women and recognizes both cognitive and affective outcomes
- Taking adequate legislative, financial and economic measures and by implementing social policies to ensure women's successful participation in adult education through the removal of obstacles and the provision of supportive learning environment
- Educating women and men in such a way as to promote the sharing of multiple workloads and responsibilities
- Encouraging women to organize as women to promote a collective identity and to create women's organizations to bring about change (ICAE, 1997)

The beauty and uniqueness of these strategies is the emphasis on male-female partnership in the process of women's empowerment. These are approaches that do not ignore the crucial role of men. Coming from a gender perspective, the strategies for promoting equality and women's integration *highlights the partnership between the two sexes and support they need from each other.*

The areas of priority outlined in the *Agenda for the Future* and the *Hamburg Declaration of Adult Education* [*which* could also form the focus of Adult Education at the international level] have revealed the multi-focused nature of the discipline. Thus Adult Education must not only have a multidimensional approach but must re-invent itself to respond to current trends and changing developments. This dynamism in Adult Education makes it a consistently powerful tool for development in our ever-changing world. The outlined areas of focus at the international forum also help to conceptualise the discipline, define its scope and ensure its applicability to national and international development.

Adult Education is not only an instrument for promoting basic literacy but a discipline for promoting all forms of education which targets the adult population and seeks to empower the marginalised for development. As a tool to promote development, the content of Adult Educational programs could range from preventive healthcare, economic empowerment, and environmental sustainability, and education for the promotion of peace.

As a commitment to the Agenda, a three-year strategic implementation plan was set forth by International Council of Adult Education to implement, monitor, follow-up and track results for further improvement. To advance adult learning at the international level, UNESCO was tasked to play a leading, proactive role within its relevant fields of action as well as and with other organizations, networks and women's organizations and other relevant participants. Following up on this, ICAE commissioned a study, *Agenda for the Future – Six Years Later,* to undertake a systematic review of CONFINTEA V, to report on the expected development on the right to learn of adults.

On the issue of gender, the study revealed that there are still gender gaps (women greatly outnumber men among the illiterate population). This called for e-strategizing in women's integration and empowerment and as a result the following strategies were outlined by the Council:

- The building of political will among decision-makers
- Development of holistic, comprehensive adult educational programmes relating to literacy/post literacy opportunities to a multi-dimensional vision of development
- Ensuring gender justice in all areas of adult learning
- supporting women's groups in their autonomous contribution to the construction of a fair and sustainable learning society
- Implementation of an affirmative action
- Assessment of budget allocations for non-formal programs especially in gender and rural urban context among others

These resolutions have trickled down to developing nations. Despite the bottlenecks that emerge from existing socio-cultural systems, the tremendous attention and resources that have been committed to the enhancement of women have advanced the women's agenda in several nation states.

The most recent Conference held in June 2004 at Gaborone under the theme, *Adult Education and Poverty Reduction: a Global Priority* raised the profile of adult education and its multifaceted potential to contribute to global poverty reduction. Over the past decade there have been a number of interventions relating to education for all; human rights; population and development; women; human settlements, and sustainable development. Meanwhile a Catch 22 situation exists; poverty is a barrier to accessing education and is exacerbated by insufficient education. Acknowledging that 70% of the world's poor are women, other marginalised people such as indigenous peoples, people with disabilities, migrant and immigrant peoples and people infected with HIV/AIDS also suffer disproportionately from poverty. Conference therefore declared that adult education at all levels is an essential element both to compensate for earlier educational inadequacies and to empower people with the necessary knowledge, understanding and skills for sustainable participation in a constantly changing world.

This review has shown that Adult Education has not been silent on broad issue of facilitating development through lifelong learning and the specific issue of promoting the gender and development. Counting women among the marginalised in society and the 50+% of the world population whose full participation is essential to holistic development, Adult Educators have since strategized to improve the lives of the world's women. Though results have not been great as expected, the tremendous improvement from Adult Educational efforts cannot be underestimated. *For no matter how it is perceived, education has emerged as the most useful tool for women's empowerment.*

CONCLUSION

Adult education is multi-focused and multi-dimensional. Though adult education began as a discipline for the of cultural transmission and the promoting of literacy and liberal education among adults, the changing nature of society has led to a widening of its scope to include *all forms of learning* among adults including higher degree programs for professional enhancement. Recognizing the strength of using education as a tool for poverty reduction (and for that matter, development), the previous Conferences have focused on adult education for development and poverty reduction. Plans have been drawn for improving the status of the marginalized in society, including women. Issues emerging from Conferences indicate that the promotion of adult learning in its multi-purposed nature will help develop individual capacity for the advancement of national development. In this process, the support of multi-lateral and bi-lateral, and governmental and non-governmental bodies must continue to be implored is set targets are to be achieved.

5
WOMEN'S EMPOWERMENT

INTRODUCTION

Attempts to empower women have travelled through decades. The year 2005 marked the:

- 10th anniversary of the Fourth World Conference on Women
- 30th anniversary of the First World Conference on Women
- 60th anniversary of the 1945 United Nations Charter which enshrined "the equal rights of men and women" in its preamble
- 10-year review of the World Programme of Action for Youth to the Year 2000 and Beyond

The year 2005 also followed closely after the 10-year anniversary of the 1994 International Conference on Population and Development that reaffirmed gender equality and reproductive health and rights as cornerstones of sustainable development. Again the year 2005 began the 10-year countdown to the 2015 deadline for achieving the Millennium Development Goals. (UNFPA, 2005)

Governments and development agencies have made considerable efforts at empowering women. Of special mention is the establishment of the Millennium Development Goals (MDGs) to address women's needs and their exclusion from the benefits of development. It is explained under the third goal of the MDGs (in regard to promoting gender equality and empowering women) that women make an enormous impact on the well-being of their families and societies; meanwhile their potential is not realized because of discriminatory social norms, incentives, and legal institutions. (WBG http://ddp-ext.worldbank.org/ext /MDG/home Date Accessed 09/09/05). The understanding is that when discriminatory burdens are removed, the capacity and earning power of women increase. Women then reinvest these gains in the welfare of their children and families, thereby multiplying their contributions to national development. Empowering women also propels countries forward towards the MDGs and improves the lives of all. Using approaches such as mainstreaming, capacity building and empowerment, strategic interventions are increasingly being adopted to bridge the gender divide under the broad framework of the MDGs. This chapter takes a critical look at the women's empowerment concept.

THE WOMEN'S EMPOWERMENT CONCEPT

In the past 30 years - from the First World Conference on Women (1975), throughout the Decade for Women (1976 - 1985), and continuing until now, there has been a great deal of debate about what constitutes the most effective strategies and approaches for supporting gender equality. In the period since the Fourth World Conference on Women (Beijing, 1995), there has been a particular focus on two approaches: women's empowerment and gender mainstreaming. Another important area of focus has been capacity-building for institutions in order to enable them to incorporate a gender equality perspective in their work.

Women's empowerment is both an approach and a goal. The Empowerment approach is articulated by Third World women. Its purpose is to empower women through greater self-reliance. Women's subordination is experienced not only because of male oppression but also because of colonial and neo-colonial oppression. The approach recognizes the triple role of women and seeks to meet strategic gender needs indirectly through bottom-up mobilization of practical gender needs.

The women's empowerment strategy emphasizes the importance of addressing years of discrimination against women by devising programmes and strategies that increase women's skills, capacities, rights, and opportunities. It addresses ways in which women can become the agents of their own development and empowerment. It thus emphasizes sustainability as well as ensuring that women feel that they have been the agents of the transformation, and have won this new space for action themselves. The empowerment promotes participatory forms of development and moves by donor agencies to embrace NGOs as partners in development. Women's advocates have emphasized that empowerment cannot be accomplished from the outside, "it is something women need to do for themselves". It is misleading to assume that governments or other external agents can empower women. As both a process and a goal, women's empowerment is fundamentally connected to democratization, human rights and the self determination of women and men.

Private researchers, donor literature, policy documents and several other literatures have shared views on women's empowerment. Karl M. [1995] remarks that long before the word became popular, women were speaking about gaining control over their lives and participating in decisions that affected them in the home and the community, in government and international development policies. She adds that the word empowerment captures this sense of gaining control, and of participating in decision-making. In defining the term empowerment, Karl (1995:14) explains what power means to her as:

- Having control, or gaining further control
- Having a say and being listened to
- Being able to define and create from a woman's perspective
- Being able to influence social choices and decisions affecting the whole society
- Being recognized and respected as equal citizens and human beings with a contribution to make

Similarly, Mbuewe and Keller (1998:190) provide a definition of women's empowerment as "a process whereby women become able to organize them-selves to increase their own self-reliance, to assert their independent right to make choices and to control resources which will assist in challenging and eliminating their own subordination". Women's empowerment could therefore be explained as the process of improving the human capital of women for effec-tive participation in all aspects of development of a nation. This will in turn help women become makers of development and history, not just recipients or ob-jects of it. Women need not be just objects or beneficiaries of development. However, the development process requires the equal participation of women as well. Recognizing that women form over 50% of the world population, their capacity building is crucial for holistic development. Women's empowerment could also be said to comprise building their capacity or making the best of the lives of women for governance and socio-economic advancement.

It is discussed in an ILO training manual that the women's empowerment strategy emphasizes the importance of addressing years of discrimination against women by devising programmes and strategies that increase women's skills, capacities, rights, and opportunities. It addresses ways in which develop-ment cooperation initiatives help create the conditions whereby women can be-come the agents of their own development and empowerment. It thus empha-sizes the transformatory potential of development initiatives - in terms of sustainability, as well as ensuring that women feel that they have been the agents of the transformation, that they have won this new space for action themselves. There has been an increased popularity of the empowerment concept which re-flects the shift away from top-down planning towards more participatory forms of development and moves by donor agencies to embrace other partners of de-velopment like Non-Governmental Organisations (NGOs) and project benefici-aries as partners in development (ILO, 2006).

If empowerment is the ability to exercise power, then everyday forms of women's empowerment are the ability of women to exercise power in the social institutions that govern their daily lives, e.g. at the level of the household and extended family; local community councils and associations; local elite; local markets and local government. Women's advocates have emphasized that em-powerment cannot be done from the outside. Thus it is something women need to do for themselves. It is therefore misleading to assume that governments or other external agents can empower women.

One aspect of empowerment is women's participation in formal political structures. This was recognized in one of the critical areas of concern in the Beijing Platform for Action, 'women in power and decision-making.' However, it seeks to identify power less in terms of domination over others (with its implicit assumption that a gain for women implies a loss for men), and more in terms of the capacity of women to increase their own self-reliance and internal strength.

As both a process and a goal, women's empowerment is fundamentally connected to democratization, human rights and the self determination of women and men. It is obvious that access to literacy or education, information or knowledge resources, natural or material resources, productive skills and capital facilitate the empowerment of women.

It could also be observed that since tradition die hard, culture, tradition, formed opinions and perceptions combine to define a marginalized status for women in society. Efforts will therefore have to be made to transform the patriarchal society through conscientization and awareness creation. In this process tradition, structures, institutions and ideologies that have contributed to the discrimination and subordination of women will have to be challenged. Some of these traditions and structures include the extended family, caste system, ethnicity, religion, the media, the law, policies and top-down development approaches as against bottom-up or participatory approaches among others.

Rowlands (1998) has explained the term in a more elaborate and practical manner, which, for the purpose of this discussion and a better understanding of the concept, is worth considering. According to Rowlands (1998), since the word 'empowerment' is built around the notion of power, a brief detour into the nature of power is necessary. The dominant understanding of power has been of 'power over' and empowerment has often been used in this sense. It is upon this definition that development discourse and the Women in Development (WID) perspectives were drawn. The view is that women should somehow be 'brought into development and become empowered' to participate within the economic and political structures of society. They should be given the chance to occupy positions of 'power' in terms of political and economic decision-making.

This view of empowerment is consistent with the dictionary definition of the term, which focuses on delegation, thus on power as something which can be bestowed by one person upon another.

As observed by Rowlands, the difficulty with this view of empowerment is that if it can be bestowed, it can just as easily be withdrawn i.e. it does not involve a structural change in power relations and is therefore illusory. Women's 'empowerment' is, in this sense, an instrumentalist discourse, where the placing of emphasis on women becomes a means to a particular end. Empowerment in this 'power over' model is in infinite supply; if some people have more, others have less. Therefore if empowerment is 'power over' then it is easy to see why it is that the notion of women becoming empowered could be seen as inherently threatening. The assumption has been that there will be some kind of reversal of relationships, and people currently in positions of power will face not only losing that power, but the possibility of having power wielded over them in turn. This perception gives the indication that behind most attempts to increase women's power is the assumption that power is a limited quantity. Thus when one individual or group gets more, the others get less. Power over is thus based on socially sanctioned threats of violence and intimidation and invites active and passive resistance and requires constant vigilance to maintain. Townsend (1999) also argues that 'power over' is exercised particularly by men and groups of men. She notes that men's power over women is the great motor which achieves and maintains the subjugation and exclusion of women found in so many societies. In some cases, this power is established through force or threats but is more subtle.

Men's fear of losing control has been an obstacle to women's empowerment. This perception about women's empowerment did not gain the support of men who mostly felt threatened that their power was being taken from them to be given to women. Some gender advocates shared this perception and adopted advocacy approaches that seemed like men wielded all the power in society, including that of women and therefore had to release some of it for women. Obviously these perceptions affected the process of WID approaches until the refocusing and re-strategising to adopt the GAD approaches.

Rowlands explains further that power can take other forms e.g. 'power to' 'power with' and 'power from within' all of which allow the construction of a very different meaning or set of meanings for 'empowerment'. To Rowlands, a feminist model of power would incorporate a gender analysis of power relations that includes an understanding of how 'internalised oppression' places internal barriers to women's exercise of power, thereby contributing to the maintenance of inequality between men and women. As cited by Rowlands (1998), for Radike and Stam "power is the capacity to have an impact or produce an effect" so that power is both the source of oppression in its abuse and the source of emancipation in its use. Therefore different types of exercise of power include 'power over' as controlling power, which may be responded to with compliance, or resistance which weakens process of victimization or manipulation, and 'power to' as generative or productive power or ability to do, which creates new possibilities and actions without domination. This refers to the individual aspect of empowerment which is creative and enabling. Some analysts also identify 'power with' which 'involves a sense of the whole being greater than the sum of the individuals, especially when a group tackles problems together". The 'power with' generates from participation in group activities which, over the years served as a great resource for women's training and capacity building. Collectively, people feel empowered through being organized and united by a common purpose or understanding, especially when a group tackles problems together. This creates energy greater than the sum of its parts.

There is also 'power from within', which refers to the spiritual strength and uniqueness that resides in each one and makes one truly human. This type of power resides within the individual and represents internal/spiritual strength. Its basis is self-acceptance and self respect which extend, in turn, to respect for and acceptance of others as equals.   Srilatha Batliwala (1993) and Kaabeer (1994) write that the power from within must be self generated, and is the fundamental power on which women must build the foundation of an answer to the powers of patriarchy and capitalism over them. This power can be what enables the individual to hold to a position or activity in the face of overwhelming opposition, or to take a challenging risk.

Rowlands concepts reveal that empowerment is not simply restricted to the 'power over' form of power, but can also involve the development of power 'to', 'with' and from 'within'. These kinds of power are not finite. Probably the more they are exercised the more power can grow. A group of people developing or exercising power of this kind does not necessarily reduce the power of others; it becomes generative power rather than controlling power.

Rowlands (1998) model of empowerment helps to deepen ones understanding of the term in a more development sense. Rowlands explains that empowerment is a complete phenomenon and takes different forms in different 'spaces' of women's lives. The process of empowerment for individual women is a personal and unique experience.   Personal empowerment involves very distinct processes from those which comprise empowerment in a group or collective sense. The process of empowerment for women in terms of their closest personal relationships, in particular with husbands and immediate family members, can be differentiated from the personal and collective experiences. These distinctions between personal and collective empowerment and empowerment in close relationships are necessary and helpful when thinking further about processes of empowerment and how to approach a conceptualisation which might serve a practical purpose in organizational and planning terms.

Empowerment can be seen to happen because changes over time gives women more access to power in one or more of its forms. For example, there are instances of women increasing their ability to act; perceive themselves as capable; hold opinions; use time effectively; control resources; interact with others; initiate activities and respond to events. These instances of power to, power with, and power from within and on occasion, power over, are significant. They demonstrate the product of empowerment processes, i.e. the evidence that empowerment has been taking place.

In order for these to happen there appear to be a core set of necessary elements, which Rowlands (1998) identifies as in Table 6.1.

Table 6.1

Personal empowerment	Collective empowerment
▪ Self-confidence	▪ Group identity
▪ Self-esteem /Dignity	▪ Collective sense of agency
▪ Sense of agency	▪ Group dignity
▪ Sense of 'self' in a wider context	▪ Self organisation and management

Any individual or group will have a history and prior experience and may therefore already have some of any of these elements, but their increase in some way is the issue. This increase needs to be in all the elements. As an element of the core of empowerment, dignity implies self-respect, self-worth, honor and the expectation of receiving and of having the right to receive respect from others. The core of the empowerment process in the area of close relationships has been identified to be slightly different, because to achieve empowerment in this area of one's life, some personal empowerment is necessary. It can be seen as an area of change arising from personal empowerment process. These are the core empowerment concepts Rowlands identifies:

Empowerment in Close Relationships:

- Ability to negotiate
- Ability to communicate
- Ability to get support
- Ability to defend self/rights
- Sense of 'self' in the relationship
- Dignity

(Rowlands, 1998:24)

These core processes of empowerment make it possible to analyze any given situation and organize things in such a way as to support empowerment processes, either by increasing the strength or likelihood of the 'encouraging elements, or by reducing, avoiding or counteracting the 'inhibiting' elements. It is observed that one person's 'empowerment' process may be another person's 'disempowerment', either because they share some situation where their two sets of needs are incompatible, or because similar processes acting in different contexts or within different power relationships have diverse impacts. Thus that which impedes empowerment for some can encourage it for others. Therefore, for the individual woman (or group) , an empowerment process will take a form which arises out of her entire environment, exposure and orientation which includes particular cultural, ethnic, historical, economic, geographic, political and social location; her place in the life-cycle, her specific life experience and out of the interaction of all these with the gender relations that prevail around her.

Karl Marilee (1995) shares a point of support to f Rowlands (1998) view; empowerment is a process, and is not therefore something that can be given to people. The process of empowerment is both individual and collective, since it is through involvement in groups that people most often begin to develop their awareness and ability to organise to take action and bring about change. Women's empowerment can therefore be viewed as a continuum of several interrelated and mutually reinforcing components. It is not static, but an ongoing process which only women can do for themselves with the support of men and entire society.

FEATURES/INDICATORS/DIMENSIONS OF WOMEN'S EMPOWERMENT

Karl, M. (1995) provides the following characteristic features of women's empowerment which help to assess any intervention to know the extent to which it could contribute to women's empowerment. These include:

- Awareness building about women's situation, discrimination, and rights and opportunities as a step towards gender equality. This implies that collective awareness building provides a sense of group identity and the power of working as a group
- Capacity building and skills developments especially the ability to plan, make decisions, organise, manage and carry out activities, to deal with people and institutions in the world around them
- Participation and greater control and decision-making power in the home, community and society
- Participation in politics either through electoral politics, public life or, non-governmental organisations and movements
- Action to bring about greater equality between men and women

It appears that these indicators are missing of economic independence. Also it does not take note of the influence which religion and social systems have on women's empowerment. Further indicators will be needed to measure women's control over religious and socio-cultural influence and economic independence. Stromquist (1993 cited in Lephoto 1995) expands the women's empowerment scope in which she adds the economic dimension. Stromquist sees empowerment as a four dimension typology.

1. *Cognitive* empowerment involves understanding of the subordinate conditions and their causes at both the micro and macro level of life. One area of concern under cognitive empowerment is knowledge about patriarchal control including sexuality and abuse in its various forms. Another important concern is the issue of legal rights.
2. *Psychological* empowerment is concerned with people's feelings and belief that they can change their situation themselves. This is one of the difficult dimensions especially for women and it requires a lot of time investment because it involves de-socialisation of the adult women. Through socialisation some African women are taught to be submissive, to be always in the background and let the males in their lives take command of all decisions.
3. *Economic* empowerment involves the ability for women to engage in income generating activities that will enable them to have access to independent income. Experience has shown that financial dependence is

one of the key sources of subordination for women. It is important for women to have access to their own income either through income generating activities or paid labour as this leads to the ability to employ a house help and thus ease some of the work burden and participate in the decision making process. At the micro level women are able to decide on the welfare of the family and especially their nutrition, health, family planning and education. Participation in decision making however small, leads to increased self-confidence and self-worth. At the macro level, participation in income earning helps open new social space where women can meet with other women who are similarly situated. This facilitates discussions on issues of mutual concern and consequently provides a fertile environment for collective action.

4. Political empowerment is the last dimension in the empowerment model that leads to political and collective awareness. While the dimensions of cognitive, psychological and economic empowerment involve critical awareness, action and change at the personal level, *political* empowerment necessarily demands extending action and change to a macro level. Through engaging in collective action women can raise cultural awareness among men and other women and therefore influence change at the social level.

Empowerment requires change at both the micro and macro level. Although women are aware of their subordination and engage in survival strategies to counter the domination and control from patriarchy, in most cases such strategies do not lead to long-term change. They are not aimed at meeting the structural gender needs. This dimension has been highlighted as very critical in other situations in order to promote change beyond the individual level. (Moser 1993 cited in Lephoto 1995; Rothschild 1989, Sanchez 1993 cited in Lephoto 1995).

THE WOMEN'S EMPOWERMENT FRAMEWORK

Sara Hlupekile Longwe, a gender expert from Lusaka, Zambia, has developed a women's empowerment framework. The purpose of the framework is to achieve women's empowerment by enabling women to achieve equal control over the factors of production and participate equally in the development process. Longwe argues that poverty arises not from lack of productivity but from oppression and exploitation. She conceptualises five progressive levels of equality, arranged in hierarchical order, with each higher level denoting a higher level of empowerment. These she explains as the basis to assess the extent of women's empowerment in any area of social or economic life.

The five levels include welfare, access; conscientisation and participation and control. These levels reflect the various approaches that have been used to promote the empowerment of women over the years.

The first level, welfare, addresses the basic needs of women. It pertains to level of material welfare of women, relative to men, with respect to food supply, income and medical care, without reference to whether women are themselves the active creators and producers of their material needs. This approach has been viewed as a top down approach. It does not recognize or attempt to solve the underlying structural causes which necessitate provision of welfare services. At this point women are merely passive beneficiaries of welfare benefits. It is obvious that such an approach promotes dependence on the provider.

Access, the second level involves equality of access to resources, such as education, opportunities, land, credit training, marketing facilities, and all publicly available services and benefits on an equal basis with men. Equality of access is obtained by securing equality of opportunity through legal reform to remove discriminatory provisions. This level is essential for women to make meaningful progress. The path to empowerment is initiated when women recognize their lack of access to resources as a barrier to their growth and over-all well being and take action to address it.

Conscientisation, the third level, is a crucial point in the empowerment framework. It is about an understanding of the difference between sex roles and gender roles and the belief that gender relations and the gender division of labour should be fair and agreeable to both sides, and not based on the domination of one over the other. For women to take appropriate action to close gender gaps or gender inequalities there must be recognition that their problems stem from inherent structural and institutional discrimination. They must also recognize the role they can often play in reinforcing the system that restricts their growth.

Participation, the fourth level is the point when women are taking decisions alongside men to ensure equity and fairness. It implies women's equal participation in the decision-making process, policy-making, planning and administration. In development projects, it includes involvement in needs assessment, project design, implementation and evaluation. This more or less re-echoes the mainstreaming approach. To reach this level, mobilisation is necessary. By organizing themselves and working collectively in groups, as expressed by Rowlands (1998) in the 'power with' notion, women become empowered to gain increased representation, which will lead to increased empowerment and ultimately greater control. This level reinforces the mainstreaming approach which proposes that the concerns of both men and women be recognized and integrated into all plans, policies, programmes, goals, objectives, activities, and monitoring and evaluation indicators. This implies that in all interventions, implications for women and men should be assessed in all areas at all levels. Another implication also is that though there might be the need for special programmes to bridge existing gaps, this should be for a period of time in a project's life cycle in order to avoid creating another imbalance.

In the framework, control is presented as the ultimate level of equity and empowerment. It is about using the participation of women in the decision-making process to achieve balance of control between men and women over the factors of production, without one in a position of dominance. At this stage women become able to make decisions over their lives and the lives of their children, and play an active role in society and the development process. Further, the contributions of women become fully recognized and rewarded as such. This level may sound like the 'power over' notion as expressed by Rowlands but a critical study will show that the control level of the framework is emphasising the 'power to' perception. It seeks to balance the share of power in society which does not mean reducing or taking the power of men but entreating and supporting women to re-generate their inhibited power or capacities.

Obviously the framework has some potential limitations. It's been observed that the assumption of levels of equality as strictly hierarchical is questionable. The framework also appears static and takes no account of how situations change over time. Again it examines gender relations from the point of view of equality alone, excluding interrelationship between rights, and responsibilities and also ignores other forms of inequality (ILO 2006). However, one could appreciate that the framework is strong in showing that empowerment is an essential element of development and enables assessment of interventions along this criterion. It also has a strong political perspective and aims to change attitudes.

CONCLUSION

The women's empowerment concept is broad. As discussed above, several scholars like Rowlands (1998); Karl Marilee (1995); Stromquist (1993 cited in Lephoto 1995) and Sara Hlupekile Longwe (in ILO 2006), have helped to develop the concept. These help to conceptualize the term and appreciate how they could be used to improve the lot of women in a holistic manner. The exciting thing about the women's empowerment framework is that it emerged from an African perspective and thus gives the African version and approach for bridging the gender divide. Rowland's theory of *power to, power with* and *power from within* helps us to acquire a better view of the different and possible interpretations of power. It also helps to know how the empowerment concept could be misused or misunderstood and for that matter affect the goal. The caution is that advocates will have to take note of these possible interpretations and implications and adopt a strategic and diplomatic approach in their work. The next chapter explores the various women's empowerment approaches in detail.

6
POLICY APPROACHES AND IMPLEMENTATION STRATEGIES FOR WOMEN'S EMPOWERMENT

INTRODUCTION

In the process of promoting women's empowerment, several policy approaches and implementation strategies have been used. These include Women in Development (WID), Women and Development (WAD), Gender and Development (GAD) and Gender Mainstreaming (GM). To a certain extent, these approaches addressed some of the gender-based contradictions in the development process. However, these WID, WAD or GAD strategies that shaped policy interventions and informed scholarly reflections in the 1960s and 1970s were limited by the fact that they remained within the established parameters of the state-led model of development and the discourses of its organic intellectuals (CODESRIA, 2005). A critical look at the various approaches will show that in the past 35+ years (from the First World Conference on Women [1975], throughout the Decade for Women [1976 – 1985] and continuing until now), there has been a great deal of debate about what constitutes the most effective implementation strategies and approaches for supporting gender equality. It could be observed that in the period since the Fourth World Conference on Women (Beijing, 1995), there has been a particular focus on two approaches: gender mainstreaming and women's empowerment. Another important area of focus has been capacity-building for institutions in order to enable them to incorporate a gender equality perspective in their work. This Chapter discusses the various policy and implementation approaches that have been emphasized over the past decades and the challenges that have emerged.

WOMEN IN DEVELOPMENT (WID) APPROACH

In the early 1970s, researchers began focusing on the gender-based division of labor and the differential impact of development and modernization strategies on women and men. And it was during this period that the term *Women in Development* (WID) came into use. In general, WID is concerned with the unequal or disadvantaged position of women as compared to men, and WID focuses on the development of strategies to minimize the disadvantages of women and end discrimination against them. Research on women (WID studies) resulted in recognition that women's experience of development and social change differed from that of men, and that women were increasingly losing out as new opportunities, training and technologies were directed almost exclusively at men. This new view was more and more supported by development agencies, and it became legitimate to focus specifically on women's experiences and perceptions.

The WID approach was institutionalized in governments and development agencies during the UN Decade for Women, from 1976 - 1988. By the end of the UN Decade for Women, the WID Policy had become an institutionalized aspect of most NGOs, and national governments had official programs for women's advancement. As stated by Debyshire (1999), the WID policies were chiefly concerned with *integrating* women into development and were aimed at providing new opportunities by which women could develop skills. The WID approach emphasized projects and programs targeting women as a group, supporting groups run by and for women, and projects and programs concerned with women's productive rather than their domestic role, thus moving away from the notion that women contribute to development only in their roles as wives and mothers.

The policy-makers felt that this was a chance for women to catch up and become integrated in development. As stated by Karl (1995), the policy-makers assumed that the neglect of women could be remedied and their situation improved by including them in development projects and programs. The main manifestation of the WID policies was a proliferation of women's ministries and units largely concerned with developing projects for women. The principal focus was women's income generation, and more recently, micro credit projects.

Moser Caroline, cited in Karl (1995), has advanced a framework where three WID policy approaches can be identified. These include equity, anti-poverty and efficiency. However she cites "welfare" as the earliest approach towards women and development. According to her, the welfare approach is a residual model of social welfare employed under the colonial administration's modernization, accelerated growth and the economic development model. This approach became very popular in 1950 – 70, and it is still widely used. Its purpose is to bring women into development as mothers, which is considered to be their most important role in development. As a result, it was strategized to meet practical gender needs in reproductive roles, goals relating particularly to food aid, malnutrition, and family planning.

The problem with this approach is that it viewed women as passive benefi-ciaries of development which focused on their reproductive role. It was non-challenging and was widely popular with government and traditional NGOs.

The equity approach, which according to Moser is the original WID ap-proach, became most popular in the years 1975 - 1985. Its purpose was to gain equity for women in the development process. The policy viewed women as active participants in development. The approach met strategic gender needs in terms of a triple role: working directly through the state, creating top-down in-terventions, and giving political and economic autonomy by reducing inequality with men.

A critical analysis of this approach will reveal that in identifying the subor-dinate position of women in terms of relationship to men, it became challenging. It has also been criticised as being a form of western feminism and was thus considered threatening and therefore not popular with governments.

In the face of this opposition the equity approach was largely abandoned and replaced with the anti-poverty approach. This policy, which developed dur-ing the 1970's, linked the economic equality of women to poverty rather than to female subordination. It was directed to the poorest of the poor and targeted low-income women through economic activity, usually small-scale income-generating projects.

It has been observed that this approach isolated poor women as a separate category, with a tendency only to recognise productive roles. Reluctance of gov-ernments to give limited aid to women meant the popularity of this approach remained at small-scale NGO level.

The third WID approach is *Efficiency,* which seeks to address deterioration in the world economy and focuses on policies of economic stabilization. Ad-justment relies on women's economic contribution to development. In this pol-icy women were seen entirely in terms of delivery capacity and ability to extend the working day, and this policy presumed that women were underused labor forces which could be exploited at a lower cost.

There are limitations within the entire WID approach, yet some of its concepts are worth noting. For example, as it is explained in a Modular Training Package of ILO, in its early days, the WID approach was closely linked to modernization strategies, which assumed that development took place in an automatic manner. The WID approach focused on the integration of women into ongoing develop-ment strategies, which entailed the acceptance of existing social structures, and on increasing the productive aspect of women's work. Women's issues were relegated to marginal programs and projects, but did not specifically address overall development activities. This is what the mainstreaming approach now seeks to address.

Academic gender analysts also found that WID interventions were doing very little to improve the status of women. The income generation programs were found to be unsuccessful and ineffectual in bringing about any sustained impact on women's lives. Artificially isolating women as a group, it assumed that all women have the same needs, and failed to recognize the interrelation of women and men's needs .

In Karl (1995), Moser takes a critical look at the WID approach and enumerates a number of problems that hindered its ability to enhance women's empowerment. According to Moser:

- None of the WID approaches questioned the model of development based on economic growth.
- The WID approach was determined by male policy makers and planners with little input from women.
- The approach fails to challenge the prevailing development model.
- It views women as an untapped labor force which could be tapped to stimulate economic growth.
- It focuses on paid employment for women without taking into consideration the enormous amount of unpaid work women were doing.
- Its interventions are seen to be top-down.
- It fails to include women's perspectives in planning and policy-making.

Ironically, most of the attempts to integrate women in development resulted instead in their marginalization. The fostering of small-scale, income-generating activities in handicrafts or fields of work considered to be women's traditional tasks, such as sewing and knitting, ignored the fact that the main activity of rural women was agricultural production. In effect, the workload of already over-burdened women was increased. Few of these projects were economically viable, and too little attention was given to training in the areas of financial accounting, management and marketing. Introduction of new and appropriate technologies, which could have alleviated women's work burden, and the provision of essential inputs and assets, was rare. However, some of these projects did provide women with opportunities to come together and develop organizing skills.

Above all, as an initial attempt to integrate women, the establishment of women's units within specialized agencies of the United Nations and women's bureau or ministries at national level was not successful. This was due to limited financial resources allocated and their lack of power to change larger policies or to influence other ministries dealing with the economy and trade. Such units marginalized women's needs and concerns, yet created the impression that they were being catered to and therefore did not have to be considered in the mainstream of development programs.

As a result of these drawbacks, parallel to the WID approach, women began to develop new visions and strategies with a view to the construction of a more people-centered development model. In 1982, the Association of African Women for Research and Development (AAWORD) issued the Dakar Declaration, stating that the most fundamental and underlying principle of another Development should be that of structural transformation at the international level.

Accordingly, the forms of dependent development and unequal terms of exchange should be replaced with that of mutually beneficial and negotiated interdependence. National models of development had to be based on the principle of self-reliance and the building of genuinely democratic institutions and practices. Such a model would ensure general participation, including that of women in the definition and actual provision of the basic needs of all citizens regardless of their race, creed, gender or age (Moser in Karl 1995; Nikoi 1998; Kwapong 2005).

GENDER AND DEVELOPMENT (GAD)

Since the mid 1980s, the shift from the integration of women to mainstreaming has been accompanied by the shift in focus from women to gender. This new approach is referred to as Gender-and-Development (GAD).

Gender

Gender is simply defined by Karl (1995:102) as "the socially defined and constructed roles of men and women". Gender is said to be a "social construct" because it is defined, supported, and reinforced by societal structures and institutions. The word "gender" differentiates the sociologically attributed aspects of individuals' identities from the physiological characteristics of men and women. Gender has to do with how we think, how we feel, and what we believe we can and cannot do because of socially defined concepts of masculinity and femininity. Gender relates to the position of women and men in relation to each other. Gender refers to men's and women's roles and relationships in a specific society or culture. The concept is based on stereotypes of male and female behaviours that are often associated with sex. Gender roles are learned and vary among cultures and often among social groups within the same culture, according to class and ethnicity. Factors such as education, technology, and economics, and sudden crises like war and famine, cause gender roles to change. Although gender roles limit both women and men, they generally have had a more repressive impact on women and have restricted their participation in the development process (CEDPA 1996). Scott's definition of gender links gender and power, because she states that "gender is a primary way of signifying relationships of power." According to Scott, gender becomes implicated in the conception and construction of power itself, because gender references establish, to a certain extent, distributions of power; that is, differential control over, or access to, material and symbolic resources (Scott, 1986:1067). Gender roles affect the division of labour; they also affect access to and control over the allocation of resources, benefits and decision-making. This contributes to inter-dependence between women and men, which is complex, subtle, flexible, and involves power relations. It also has implications for women's income-generating opportunities. Women often have less access to resources than men, and less control over their own labour. For women, access to certain sub-sectors and sources of employment may be restricted, and support services may be harder to obtain. Women may have difficulty exercising control over their income. Gender equality gives women and men the same entitlements to all aspects of human development, including economic, social, cultural, civil and political rights; the same level of respect; the same opportunities to make choices and the same level of power to shape the outcomes of these choices.

It is generally expressed that gender is a socio-economic variable functioning to analyse roles, responsibilities, constraints, opportunities, and the needs of women and men in any context. Unlike sex, which is biologically determined, gender roles change from one place and culture to another and across time. They are learned behaviours in a given society or community that condition which activities, tasks and responsibilities are perceived as male and female. Gender roles are affected by age, class, race, ethnicity, religion and other ideologies, and by the geographical, economical and political environment. Changes in gender roles often occur in response to changing economic, natural or political circumstances. These roles may be flexible or rigid, similar or dissimilar, or may complement or conflict within a certain social context.

GENDER AND DEVELOPMENT

Rowlands (1998) remarks that GAD is an *approach* and not simply concerned with women's roles, but with the dynamics and structures of gender relations. The position of women is often characterized by multiple roles. Besides being a worker, a woman has many other roles in society, such as being a mother, wife, relative, or community member. And if, for instance, women are housewives, their assumption of this role occurs not in a vacuum but in situations in which men, other women, and society at large expect them to be housewives. The gender and development approach therefore starts from a holistic perspective, linking the relations of production to the relations of reproduction, and taking into account all aspects of women's lives.
It analyses the nature of women's economic and social contribution within the context of work done both inside and outside the household.

This gender approach is not concerned with women per se, but with the social construction of gender disparities, based on the assignment of specific roles, responsibilities and expectations to men and women, which prevent the enjoyment of equal opportunities and treatment. Therefore, in order to promote change in social, economic and political structures, women are considered to be agents of change rather than passive recipients of development assistance. The gender approach thus stresses the need for women to organize themselves and to participate in institutions and organizations side- by-side with men.

Rowlands (1998) emphasizes that GAD theorists have highlighted the value systems which lead to a gender-based division of labour, varyingly constituted, and placed emphasis on the socially-constructed nature of gender and gender relations. Since gender inequalities touch all aspects of women's lives, GAD also requires the inclusion of all aspects of women's lives within the ambit of *relevant issues,* i.e., their physical situation; intra-household relations; health; sexuality; education and means of livelihood, etc. The approach makes visible the power relations that exist between men and women in most societies and the subordination that most women face. Elson, as quoted by Rowlands, adds that gender analysis enables a critique of the many manifestations of male bias in the development process.

In a similar vein, Debyshire (1999) expresses that GAD analysis seeks to focus on gender as opposed to women in order to draw attention to the fact that gender roles and responsibilities are not determined by biology but developed within the social context. Karl's (1995) outstanding view is that there are some who see the GAD approach as having the potential to bring in women's vision of development. In addition, the use of the term *gender* as an analytical tool offers advantages over the WID concept because it focuses not on women as an isolated group, but on the roles and needs of men *and* women. The WID concept requires input from both sides in order to effect the changes needed to achieve greater equality between men and women. The ultimate objective is the advancement of the status of women in society by giving explicit attention to women's needs, interests and perspectives.

A comparison of the WID and GAD approaches has been provided as follows:

FACTOR	WID	GAD
The approach	Views women as the problem	Emerges as an approach to development
The focus	Women	Relations between men and women
The problem	Exclusion of women/ disadvantaged situation of women in development process	Unequal relations of power and status that prevent equitable development/full participation
The Goal	More efficient effective development	Equitable, sustainable developm ent with men and women as decision-makers
The solution	Integrate women into existing development process	Empower the disadvantaged including women to transform the influencing factors and relations
The strategies	Women's projects, components, integrated projects, increase women's productivity, income and ability to look after the household	Identify/address Practical Gender Needs [PGN] as determined by women and men to improve their condition. At the same time address women's strategic interests and that of the poor through people-centred development.

Source: Two Halves make a Whole, CCIC, 1992

A major difference is that, while WID is women-specific, GAD focuses on the social relations between men and women and its implications for development.

The GAD approach has some noticeable drawbacks as well. According to Karl (1995), like WID, the GAD approach does not question the prevailing development paradigm per se, rather its potential to do so depends on how it is interpreted and applied. In Ghana, a study by Advocates for Gender Equity (AGE) on Gender Mapping Exercise (2000) concluded that in its movement towards the GAD approach, the status of Ghana has not lent itself to an easy assessment for three main reasons, which include:

1) The absence of national policy framework to engender equity issues
2) A strong women's improvement
3) A fragmented database on gender activities in the country

Debyshire (1999) also remarks that the transition from WID to GAD is also more evident in theory than in practice.

In view of the above limitations, the Advocates for Gender Equity's study on Gender Mapping Exercise (2000) recognized the need to develop a network of programs and managers/resource persons involved in gender and development activities for the purpose of building their capacity to spearhead the change from WID to GAD activities. Recent developments have also included the need to mainstream gender in all interventions, policies and implementation, to enforce existing laws, and to generate gender-disaggregated data for decision/policy making.

MAINSTREAMING

The ultimate goal of mainstreaming is to achieve gender equality. Mainstreaming focuses on the institutional arrangements and responsibilities for operationalizing a gender approach to development and is an integral part of the gender approach to development. A gender mainstreaming strategy emphasizes the importance of addressing the different impacts and opportunities that a particular program or policy may have on women and men. The strategy focuses on making gender equality concerns central to policy formulation, legislation, resource allocation, and planning and monitoring of programs. Using a gender mainstreaming strategy to achieve gender equality requires changes in the awareness and capacity of all personnel and implies strong management commitment. Gender mainstreaming strategies have obtained high priority in the Beijing Platform for Action.

Debyshire (1999) notes that the term "gender-mainstreaming" came into widespread use with the 1995 adoption of the Beijing Platform for Action. It entreats governments and agencies to promote mainstreaming of gender perspective in all policies and programmes. The Women Workers Rights module explains that in the late 1980s there was a shift to mainstreaming women in development approaches at all levels, from macro-level planning to micro-level projects. A mainstreaming strategy calls for introducing gender analysis and planning in all programs and projects at all stages of the development process and is characterised by a shift away from women-specific projects.

Mainstreaming includes a movement away from the concept of women and development to the concept of gender and development. In all areas and at all levels, mainstreaming is a process of assessing the implications for women and men of any planned action, including legislation, policies and programs. It is a strategy for making women's as well as men's concerns and experiences an integral dimension of the design, implementation, monitoring and evaluation of policies and programmes in all political, economic and societal spheres, so that women and men benefit equally, and so that inequality is not perpetuated.

It has been vividly explained in the Women Workers Rights Package (1994) that mainstreaming women in development denotes strengthening women's active involvement in development by linking women's capabilities and contributions with macro-economic issues such as structural adjustment, industrialization policies, critical poverty, environmental management and conservation, urbanization and privatization. Mainstreaming requires explicit consideration of the actual and potential role of women in all sectors of the economy, and the impact of all policies, plans and programs on women. Women's needs and concerns should not be marginalized as being the responsibility of only one agency/focal point or one sex. Mainstreaming does not exclude the use of women-specific activities as an alternative option, especially where women are particularly disadvantaged.

A number of strategies that have been developed to bring women into the mainstream and to make gender a central focus of development; such strategic programs include:

- Strengthening women's units, groups and organisations to ensure gender awareness, to act as pressure groups, and to monitor the implementation of mainstreaming women
- Increasing gender-awareness and analysis training
- Building a critical mass of women inside development organisations d
- Lobbying and pressuring development institutions

To Karl (1995), the combination of strategies can enable women to participate in the mainstream and empower them to determine the nature and goals of their participation. She further suggests that the majority of women's supported development institutions and research groups be established to bring pressure to bear on policy makers and create a climate for gender awareness and analysis. Openness to dialogue, collaboration, coalition building and co-ordination are the keys to success.

Touching on the limitations of mainstreaming, Debyshire (1999) acknowledges that there is no tried and tested formula for success, and that experience with gender mainstreaming is still limited. It is clear that gender mainstreaming is not easy and that considerable persistence, commitment, support and resources are required.

THE EMPOWERMENT APPROACH

The commonality of the four approaches that have been discussed is that they take little account of the historical inequalities of power between men and women in their societies. The empowerment (or autonomy) approach therefore emerged in the mid 1970s among Third World women and their organizations and is based on their experiences. It recognized that feminism is not simply a recent, western, urban, middle-class import, but has an independent history. Third World feminism has its roots in women's participation in nationalist struggles, working-class agitation and peasant rebellions. This approach has been an important source for change.

The empowerment approach's objective is to strengthen and broaden the power- base of women so that they may achieve greater self-reliance. It defines women's inequality not only as a problem in relation to men, but also in relation to their race, class, colonial history, and current position in the international economic order.

Karl (1995) shares the view that the concept of empowerment of women as a goal of development projects and programmes gained wider acceptance in the 1990s. According to Young, K., in Karl (1995), the concept of empowerment (as used by development agencies) refers mainly to entrepreneurial self-reliance. It is closely allied to the current emphasis on individualistic values, e.g., people *empowering themselves* by pulling themselves up by their bootstraps. Young continues to explain that, on the other hand, an empowerment approach to development can also mean people's participation in the policy-making and planning processes. It has been recognized in development circles that economic growth and social betterment are best achieved when the mass of the population is informed about and involved in development aims and plans, and sees itself as a direct beneficiary of the expanded resources that growth should bring. The decision-making process should ensure widespread consultation at all levels of society to determine development goals, the processes by which those goals are to be reached, and the resources needed to achieve them. Empowerment can therefore be a planning goal in the sense that government support is given to a range of interest groups and Non-Governmental Organizations by using them as consultative bodies or councils.

Karl's (1995) study identifies two approaches commonly used by development agencies:

1.   Empowerment through economic interventions to increase women's economic status through employment, income generation and access to credit

2. Empowerment through integrated rural development programmes in which strengthening women's economic status is only one component together with education, literacy, awareness creation, the provision of basic needs and services, and fertility control

Other approaches include organizing women to transform unequal decision-making power in the home and community and develop greater participation in politics. Some of these ideas have been implemented in programs to develop gender-training networks that promote the concept of empowerment.

Similarly, the empowerment approach, as elaborated in the Modular Training Package (1994), targets women as subordinate to men in all spheres. It is aimed at women's self-reliance and influence in social change. The approach refers to women's triple role, which it redefines as productive, reproductive and public, with emphasis on women's access to decision-making. Its operational strategy is given as consciousness- raising, popular education, organization and mobilisation of women, with women participating as potential actors for social change.

The main criticism identified in this empowerment approach is that it is bottom-up only and disregards the potential of public policy. Above all, Moser remarks, the empowerment approach is potentially challenging, with its emphasis on Third World and women's self-reliance, and thus it is largely unsupported by governments and agencies (cited in Karl, 1995). Again, avoidance of overt western feminism means slow (albeit significant) growth of under-financed voluntary organizations.

At the grassroots level, many development agencies have directed their programs and projects toward the empowerment of women through capacity-building and the strengthening of both women's organizations and women's participation in rural associations. Their participation in grassroots organizations is increasingly recognized as crucial to their empowerment and as a way for them to shape development policies.

IMPLICATIONS FOR TRAINING

Building the capacity of change agents is very crucial in the empowerment process, especially when this book is being written from an adult education perspective and, for that matter, a human resource development perspective. Rowlands (1998) comments that the role of change agents in programs intended to promote empowerment for women is potentially a pivotal one. In some form, change agents are usually outsiders, extension workers, or experts. The attitudes they bring to their work, and the forms their work takes, can have an immense impact (positive or negative) on the people they work with. In regard to empowerment, there are a number of attitudes and skills which are essential for change agents to have. The attitudes of the change agents should be those necessary when working with women to develop self-esteem, self-confidence, and a belief that they are competent to act in a wider sphere. For instance, the attitude of the change agent should include complete respect for each individual and for the group; humility and mutual willingness to learn; and a total commitment to the empowerment process. The skills of the change agent need to be consistent with the open-ended nature of the process, i.e., facilitation skills, active listening skills and non-directive questioning skills. This conforms to Malcom Knowles' principle of andragogy, which recognizes the concept of the learner, the role of the learner's experience, her readiness to learn, and her orientation to learning. This implies that there is the need to adopt a learner-centered approach in the teaching-learning process.

The role of the change agent is essentially one of a catalyst. All human beings are the product of their particular life history and culture. It is vital for change-agents to have self-awareness and to understand their own biases, priorities, and areas of similarity to or difference from the women with whom they are working. According to Knowles (1997) Rowlands (1998) and Bhola (2004), in view of these essential qualities change agents must possess, their training becomes an important issue. The required skills and attitudes are not easily or quickly acquired and therefore call for frequent practice and constant monitoring. Some training therefore needs to be ongoing, with many opportunities for self-evaluation and self-reflection. This may imply formal training, or may be an informal on-the-job process with constant analysis of the process, and appropriate support to combat isolation.

The methodology used in the training is also a crucial issue. There is a challenge to encourage women to set their own goals while also encouraging them to question their assumptions and those of others about what is possible. This means leaving the women in charge while at the same time challenging the internalized oppression that pushes them to accept a diminished view of their own capacity.

Karl (1995) gives some good reasons why there should be extensive and careful training for agents involved in the empowerment of women. She explains that within development organisations and the United Nations agencies, gender training aims to provide planners with an awareness of women's and men's interrelated and changing reproductive and productive roles, and equips the planners with tools designed to ensure that women are fully part of their programs and projects. This training helps planners to identify the gender roles in a given place. For instance, training may focus on what men and women do and how the two are interrelated or impact on the teaching-learning engagements, men's and women's differing access to and control over resources, and the constraints facing them. The issue that women work more hours and perform more tasks per day than men can be used in planning appropriate project interventions as well as in the allocation of project inputs, training and other benefits. Most grassroots gender awareness training has been aimed at making women aware of their own situation and subordination as a first step in the process of empowerment, while it is also used to sensitise men (Schalkwyk 1997; Group 2005; UN-FPA 2005; UNFPA 2005; UN 2006).

To achieve a high level of empowerment and realize immediate results of any empowerment intervention, training becomes an essential element. And this will not have to be a singular event, but a continuous process. In this way, professionalism in the empowerment process will not be compromised. Yes, there could be challenges, but with a high level of commitment to the task, provision of adequate training and on-the-job learning, much could be achieved.

CONCLUSION

The discussion on the approaches for women's empowerment shows how since the early 1970s the women's empowerment processes have evolved from the Welfare, Women in Development, Gender and Development to Mainstreaming and Empowerment. Specific measures by development agencies for empowering women have included activities to increase women's economic status through employment, income generation, and access to credit. There has also been empowerment through integrated rural development programmes, in which strengthening women's economic status is only one component in conjunction with education, literacy, the provision of basic needs and services, and fertility control. In recent times, focus has been on education for all, economic empowerment, integrated quality health care, inclusion in sustainable natural resource management, and full participation in governance, especially at the grass roots level.

It is obvious that these approaches overlap. However, it shows the trend of progress. In all these stages of progress there have been drawbacks and inhibiting factors which inform the strategy or the approach that follows. Notable among the inhibiting factors are the poor societal and male support, most likely due to the initial approaches to women's empowerment, the strong influence of socio-cultural factors, and discriminatory religious and social practices against women. Others inhibiting factors have included women's lack of self-confidence; low formal education and training among women; low economic status of women; and poor enforcement of existing laws. Despite the constraints and challenges which call for intensified efforts, one could say that much has been achieved towards the empowerment of women.

7
EMPOWERMENT AMONG WOMEN OF MO COMMUNITIES OF GHANA

INTRODUCTION

The Mo Traditional Area is located in the North Western corridor of Ghana in the Brong Ahafo region. The area is inhabited by small farming communities, with Ayorya, Nkwanta, Weila, New Longoro (Mantukwa), Bamboi, Busuema and Asantekwa being the notable ones. The position of the women in the Mo communities is complicated and challenging. It is reported that like most communities in developing countries, the females are more disadvantaged than the males. The Mo communities have features of a rural community as well as high population pressures, decreasing agricultural yields, land degradation and deforestation, and traditional problems with poverty and gender inequalities. Agricultural productivity is very low since subsistence farming is more or less the only choice of occupation. The women do most of the farming; they are excellent traders and run several businesses. As a result many other projects have used the Mo region women's groups for village-level activities (Ghana-Canada In-Concert, 2000; Oppong and Quashie-Sam, 2001).

This study sought to assess the level of empowerment among the women in the Mo communities of the Brong Ahafo Region of Ghana. Specific objectives were to discover

- How the respondents' bio-characteristics affect their level of empowerment
- The women's formal educational attainment
- The women's economic independence
- The extent of the women's participation in decision-making in the home
- The extent to which the women take part in decision-making in the communities.

This chapter not only shares the findings of the study but discusses observations from the findings as well.

THE SURVEY

A survey was conducted to find out the level of empowerment among the women of the Mo communities of the Brong-Ahafo Region of Ghana. It was conducted among a total of 200 women of the Mo communities. The distribution was 66 from Weila, 61 from New Longoro, 39 from Bamboi and 34 from Ayorya.

A survey instrument of five sections and 34 items was used to elicit information from the respondents. The instrument included both closed and open-ended questions. Section One was on the personal characteristics of the respondents and consisted of five items which questioned respondents on their age, level of formal education, religious affiliation, marital status and major occupation. Section Two was designed to elicit information on the respondents' level of educational empowerment and included seven items, including the influence of education on their socio-economic life, their desire for further training, and their initiatives to enhance female education. Section Three consisted of twelve items designed to test the women's level of economic empowerment and contained the most questions. The questions were based on the women's access to farmland, their income-generating activities, the influence of their spouses on their income-generating activities, and their means of saving money. Section Four was designed to determine the women's level of participation in decision-making in the home and consisted of five items. The questions concerned the women's ability to share ideas with their spouses, the type of decisions that they were able to make, and their ability to decide on their own when handing over properties to their heirs. The Fifth and final section of the survey instrument was structured with the intent of finding out the women's level of participation in decision-making in their communities and included five items. The items asked the women's affiliation to any women's organization; the benefits they derived from the associations; their ability and opportunity to express their views in public gatherings and the extent to which their views were taken seriously. The entire survey instrument included 31 closed questions and three open-ended items. While the closed questions yielded standardized responses, the open-ended items gave the women the chance to express their views in their own way. Field data was collected with the support of research assistants who were trained teachers from that locality and spoke the local language. The people were interviewed in their local dialects (Twi and Deg) to enhance accuracy of the results. In order not to inconvenience the women, the interviews were done in their various houses. This approach was mainly associated with the problem of a few interruptions from household members and customers of the traders. However, at the end of the day the researchers got the required information. The women also had the opportunity to share their experiences. The interviews lasted over a period of four weeks (28 days). The tool for the data analysis was percentages. The results were organized in tables, graphs and pie charts.

FINDINGS
Demographics of Respondents

Age of Respondents

On the age of the respondents, the results revealed that while 94% of the women were in their independent adulthood stage of development (21-60 years), only 2.6% fell within a semi dependent stage of below 21 and 61+. This implies that the subjects of the research were active persons who formed part of the working force of the community. With the majority of the respondents being in their active stage and therefore forming the labour-force of the community, their responses should depict a clear picture of the level of empowerment among the women in the Mo communities.

Formal Educational Attainment

On the participants level of formal education, as many as 33.9% of the women had no formal education at all; only 19.7% had schooled up to Senior Secondary School [SSS] level, with 64.5% ending at the Middle, Junior Secondary and Primary school levels. Only 1.6% had completed teacher training. This shows that the respondents had a very low level of formal education. Those who managed to attain some form of formal education mainly ended at the basic level. This low level of the women's formal education can affect their level of empowerment to a very high extent. Pomary explains that "No matter how much we run away from it, the foremost agent of empowerment is education: education is the only passport to liberation, to political and financial empowerment. Education contributes to sustainable development. It brings about a positive change in our lifestyles. It has the benefit of increasing earnings, improving health and raising productivity" (1999:21). It will therefore be crucial to give the women some adult literacy skills to enhance their capabilities.

Religious Affiliation

Typical of most Ghanaian communities, the majority of the respondents, 66.1%, were Christians, followed by Muslims who were 23.3%, with only 9.8% being Traditional Religious believers. This indicates that since Christians and Muslims are found to be meeting in groups for worship, a majority of the women were associated with a group. This affiliation could facilitate their empowerment to some extent. Rowlands (1998) remarks that it is through involvement in groups that people most often begin to develop their awareness and ability to take action to bring about change.

Marital Status

The importance of marriage as an institution to the Ghanaian woman (Dolphyne, F., 1998) was manifest in the results obtained on marital status of the respondents. The results showed that 77% of the women were married and 13.7% single. Owing to the value that women (and for that matter the Ghanaian society) place on marriage, only 6% were either divorced or separated, meaning that the women tried as much as possible to maintain their marriages. Thus marriage appeared significant to and well appreciated by the women. This characteristic could probably enhance empowerment in close relationships among the women, as identified by Rowlands (1998).

Occupation

The major occupation of the respondents was farming, 71%, followed by trading and engagement in other income-generating activities like pito (traditional drink) brewing and the manufacture of artefacts. Only 3.3% of the respondents were public/civil servants. The issue of unemployment was not highly prevalent among the respondents. Only 1.1% replied that they were unemployed. We can therefore establish that almost all of the women had an income generating activity, or at the very least had the means of earning their livelihood. Having gainful employment could go a very long way to facilitate the women's level of economic empowerment and decision-making, leading to a high level of independence. Asante (1978) and Oppong (1974) remark that the woman's position in decision-making has weight only when she has occupational and financial resources. Greenstreet (1978) also emphasizes that the woman's valuable economic activities enable her to enjoy a great deal of economic independence and equality.

EDUCATIONAL EMPOWERMENT

As discussed in previous chapters, women's development has been on the agenda of both development partners and governments, in recognition of the need to accelerate progress in women's development. Studies have shown that women, in comparison to men, experience greater poverty, have heavier time burdens, lower rates of utilisation of productive resources, and lower literacy rates. Gender disparities exist with respect to access to and control of a range of assets, including direct productive assets such as land and credit, and social and human capital assets such as education.

The results of the survey on the formal educational attainment of the women of Mo were not far from the broader reality, a low level of formal educational attainment among women. Research has shown that women have low literacy levels. Literate women are defined in the Ghana Living Standards Survey (GLSS 4, 2000) as those who could write a simple letter in the local or English Language. The GLSS 4 (2000) reveals that in the whole of Ghana, almost two-thirds (66%) of adults in urban areas are literate, while in rural areas only

41% are literate. The literacy rates of females ages 6 – 25 years in the Brong Ahafo region of Ghana is 61.8%, compared to a 72.6% literacy among the males. In rural Brong Ahafo, 58.4% females have been to school compared to 70.8% of males.

On general educational attainment (as explained in the GLSS 4 [2000]), about 32% of all adults (representing about three and a half million people) have never been to school. A further 25% (almost three million adults) went to school but did not obtain any qualifications. About 33% (three million and three hundred adults) have the MSLC/JSS certificate as their highest qualification, while the remaining 10% (a million adults) have secondary or higher-level qualifications. There is a marked contrast between females and males in levels of educational attainment. For instance, more than twice as many females as males (2.4 million as against 1.1 million) have never been to school; in contrast, only half as many females as males have secondary or higher qualifications (Table 1).

The results from the survey on women in the Mo communities of Brong Ahafo Region of Ghana were not much different from the observations in the GLSS 4. As many as 33.9% of the women studied had no formal education; 35.5% had had some type of formal education that ended at the basic Junior Secondary, Senior Secondary and Middle Schools level. Only 1.6% had schooled up to Teacher Training level. Most likely, completing the basic education seemed to be sufficient for the women, and as a result, almost 50% of the women rated themselves as having a low level of education, with 31.1% rating themselves at the average level. This implies that the women had not highly benefited from the current waves of advocacy and developments on female education. Although the results showed that the 94% of the women desired to promote girl-child education to a very high extent, they were not able to do very much about it, probably due to their own low level of education. Thus the results further showed that 32.8% rated themselves as averagely involved in the promotion of female education, and 36.1% rated their involvement as low.

In comparing the women's age and marital status, it was observed that all the women under age 20 were single. The married women fell between the ages of 21 and 60 (Table 2). These statistics indicate that early marriage was not prevalent among the women and therefore could not become a barrier to their education. Thus, given adequate support and motivation, and controlling or at least managing other inhibiting factors, the women could pursue higher education.

It is encouraging to note that the women had the urge to improve upon their low level of education, given that 97% of the women's responses indicated a desire to participate in further training to enhance their career, with as much as 93.4% deciding to give such a program full participation. A significant number, 94%, desired to champion the cause of girl-child education. This shows that the women saw the need to promote the formal education of their younger females to a higher level.

TABLE 1: LEVELS OF EDUCATIONAL ATTAINMENT, BY SEX, AND ESTIMATES OF EDUCATIONAL ATTAINMENT FOR THE POPULATION AGED 15 AND ABOVE

Highest level attained	Percent			Estimates (millions)		
	Male	Female	All	Male	Female	All
Never been to school	21.1	41.0	31.8	1.0	2.3	3.3
Less than MSLC/BECE	24.6	25.6	25.1	1.2	1.4	2.6
MSLC/BECE	38.6	27.8	32.8	1.8	1.5	3.3
Secondary or higher	15.8	5.7	10.4	0.7	0.3	1.0
Total	100.0	100.0	100.0	4.7	5.5	10.2

Source: Table 2.1, GLSS 4, 2000

ECONOMIC EMPOWERMENT

Data from Ghana Living Standards Survey (GLSS 4, 2000) suggest that in Ghana, out of a total population of about 14.7 million aged 7 years and above, some 11.3 million people are currently economically active, giving an economic activity rate of around 77%. It is stated that the economic activity rate for women in the age group 15-64 is lower than those for men. But in the younger age group (7-14), and the older age group (65+), the rates for females exceed those for males. Most of the adults who are classified as economically active in Ghana are employed. The employed adults in the active population total 8.3 million (4.1 million males and 4.2 million females). The GLSS 4 results on the employment status of adults show that nearly nine out of ten adults are economically active. About 4% of women and 2% of male adults have been classified as homemakers because they are not economically active but spend some time on housekeeping activities.

The GLSS 4 further reports that there appear to be differences in the employment status of adults in urban and rural areas. In urban areas, about 80% of male adults and 77% of female adults are employed, whereas in rural areas, about 84% of males and 82% of females are employed, indicating that unemployment is a significant phenomenon in urban areas but relatively small in rural areas. More than three quarters of urban workers (about 80%) are involved in non-agricultural work, but just a little over a quarter of the rural people are involved in non-agricultural activities. The distribution of males and females among the types of work indicates that more males are involved in wage employment than females, but the percentage of females in unpaid family work far exceeds the percentage of males in that activity.

TABLE 2: RELATIONSHIP BETWEEN AGE AND MARITAL STATUS OF RESPONDENTS

MARITAL STATUS

BROAD AGE GROUPS	Married		Single		Widowed		Separated		Divorced		Total	
	Freq.	%	Freq.	%	Freq.	%	Freq.	%	Freq.	%	Freq.	%
Under 20			3	1.6							3	1.6
21-40	78	42.6	17	9.3	2	1.1	1	0.5	4	2.2	102	55.7
41-60	57	31.1	5	2.7	3	1.6	2	1.1	3	1.6	70	38.3
61+					1	0.5			1	0.5	2	1.0
No response	6	3.5									6	3.3
Total	141	77	25	13.7	6	3.2	3	1.6	8	4.3	183	100.0

Source: Field Survey, 2001

It is also revealed in the GLSS 4 that almost all working women are self-employed in their main job; only about 1 in 16 women work for an employer. A large number of men are also self-employed, while approximately 1 in 4 men work for an employer. Over 90% of workers in rural areas work are self-employed (both in agriculture and non-agriculture), and also in the informal private sector. Meanwhile, in urban areas relatively more people are employed in the formal sector. In all, there are about 3.7 million employed people in the working age population whose main occupation is in agriculture. Also significant is the high proportion of women (a little over a quarter) engaged in sales or commerce, and a relatively larger proportion of men in occupations related to production. The national survey further reveals that about 70% of workers in rural areas are involved in agricultural occupations, whereas about a third of workers in urban areas are involved in commerce, with a quarter of the urban employees also involved in production.

Results from the survey on the women of the Mo communities of Ghana also showed that a majority of 71% of the women were farmers while 18% reported that they were in trading. About 11% of the women engaged in other income-generating activities like brewing of pito (local drink), catering services, and the manufacture of artefacts. Only 3.3% of the women were civil/public servants. Farming therefore happened to be the major occupation of the women. Apart from the farming, trading was the alternative for the women. The results on other sources of income showed that 68.3% of the women took trading to be their non-farming income-generating activity. This was followed by other small-scale businesses like gari-processing and shear-butter extraction, which were undertaken by 10.8% of the women Meanwhile 20.7% did nothing at all apart from the farming.

The general observation that could be made from this result is that, probably because of the women's low level of formal education, they operate mainly in the informal sector to gain their livelihood. This assertion can be buttressed with the view of Awumbila (2001) that women have low literacy levels and accompanying poor employment prospects, which has accounted for their domination of the informal sector, especially small-scale food crop farming and petty-trading. Manu (1990) endorses this view by expressing that the informal sector is considered as the key factor for the survival of a large proportion of the Ghana population, especially women. Brown (2001) however provides other reasons for this, stating that many women find it relatively easy within the informal sector to care for their children, perform domestic chores and also to engage in their numerous economic activities.

Recognising this, it will be helpful to provide incentives for the women in the informal sector towards increasing their productivity. The Government of Ghana has a development agenda to improve the informal sector. The Government seeks to undertake broad-based pro-market reforms in order to create an environment where all businesses can operate competitively, and where the private sector has the incentive to take risks, innovate and diversify. The Government also seeks to facilitate the free and fair operation of markets –

enhancing access to new entrants, reducing distortions and inefficiencies, and reducing the risks and costs of doing business in Ghana. To facilitate and support the process, the Government has launched the Presidential Special Initiatives.

It is very significant to note that the issue of unemployment does not pertain to the group of women surveyed. The unemployment rate is defined as the proportion of the economically active population who are not working but are available for work. For the country as a whole, the adult unemployment rate is 8.2%. It is lower for males (7.5%) than for females (8.7%). As suggested by data from the GLSS 4, in most rural areas unemployment rates are very low, and very little difference exists among the ecological zones. In contrast, the rates in urban areas are much higher. For example, for the age group 15-24 years, the GLSS recorded unemployment rates close to 30% in the capital city of Accra, and rates in excess of 20% for both males and females in other urban areas. Therefore unemployment in Ghana is an urban phenomenon; 13.2% of currently active urban adults are unemployed, whereas only about 4.8% of adults in rural areas are currently unemployed. Meanwhile, underemployment seems to affect people in both urban and rural areas, but it appears to be more pronounced in rural areas, where about 15% of the adult population is under-employed. Research results suggest that males and females have almost identical rates of unemployment and under-employment. The only apparent exception is found in rural areas.

Similarly, it could be observed from the results of the Survey on the women of Mo communities of Ghana that unemployment is not prevalent among the women. The results showed only 1.1% of the women were unemployed. The majority of the Mo women in this study, 98.9%, reported that they were engaged in an income-generating activity. For the vast majority of this 98%, to be engaged in income-generating activities reveals that they had a measure of economic independence. In Brown (2001), Oppong emphasizes that the majority of wives are in gainful employment, and some of those who stayed at home earned money by trading, sewing or baking. Few wives feel that they can afford to depend entirely upon their husbands for support. Bukh (1979) and Benneh (1995) explain that the influence and over-dependence on husbands are among the factors that hinder women's economic independence. However, a critical analysis of the data shows that the women are breaking free from this tradition.

When the women were questioned on their ability to mange their own income-generating activities, 97% of them said they were able to do so, indicating that they had some capabilities in their economic activities, and nearly 63% of the women expressed that they controlled their own income. Only 36% said it was their husbands who controlled or managed their income. These findings indicate that the Mo women attained a high level of economic independence. When the women were questioned on their level of dependence on their husbands, only 22% of the women said they depended highly on their husbands, and 36.3% of the women said they did not really depend on their husbands. This analysis emphasizes that the small-scale businesses of the women were able to

provide for their needs, and thus facilitate and enhance their economic independence.

Another observation that could be made from the data analysis is that,
probably because 97% of the women were able to manage their own jobs, 63%
of them were capable of controlling or managing their own incomes; 83% of the
women were allowed by their husbands to decide on how to use their money,
and 83% were also allowed by their husbands to cultivate for commercial purposes. There is a strong indication that the women had financial or economic
independence to a large extent. These observations re-echo the observations of
Greenstreet (1978) and Asante (1978), both of whom maintain that the woman's
numerous and valuable economic activities enable her to enjoy a great deal of
economic independence and equality. In addition, owing to the wife's economic
autonomy and, subsequently, her independence from the husband, the traditional
dominance and supervision of the wife by the husband are reduced. Woman's
financial contribution to the family's budget enhances her power position in the
home and therefore strengthens the woman's bargaining power.

In regard to the issue of the husbands allowing women to decide on how to
use their money, 83% of the women responded in the affirmative. However, this
response does not conform to the general view that while women are largely
responsible for generating increases in incomes, the increases are often appro-
priated by men and spent in ways that do not benefit the women or children. The
trends have changed. The results show that the women were in control of their
own income and its related activities.

In addition, when the women's extent of economic independence was cross-
tabulated with their ability to manage their own jobs (income sources), it was
clear that 78% of the women who depended on their husbands economically to
some extent were able to manage their own income-generating activities; only
1.1% of the women were not able to do likewise. This suggests that the women's
dependence on their husbands economically did not necessarily mean that they
were unable to manage their own businesses rather their economic dependence
on their husbands could be attributed to their lack of a regular source of income.
According to the results, 64% of the women who depended on their husbands
economically did not have a regular source of income.

Regarding the type of savings achieved by the women, it can be observed
that the nature of the women's occupation (which is mainly small-scale business), their state of income source, and probably their low level of education
influence their habits regarding saving. The results on savings revealed that
62.3% of the women engaged in 'suss' (saving money with individual agents)
with only 9% engaged in banking. 25% did not engage in any type of saving at
all. The women's inability to engage in banking transactions (with interest and
loan incentives) could negatively affect the growth and progress of their small-
scale businesses and impede their growth towards economic empowerment.

Another factor that could impede the progress of the women's economic
empowerment is their access to land. Although the survey results regarding
access to land suggests that nearly 88% of the women had access to land for

commercial purposes, the comparison of land owned by women to that of men revealed that 28.4% of the women's land was, on average, comparable to the land owned by men, and 22.4% of their land was small compared to that of the men. Only 28.4% of the women said their land could be favourably compared to the land owned by the average man. A contributing view with respect to the issue of land as an obstacle to women in farming is given by Awumbila (2001) and emphasized in the Women's Manifesto (2004). Awumbila posits that while women play a significant role in the national economy, their productivity is constrained by a number of factors, including limited access to and ownership of the productive resources of land, capital and credit. As expressed in the Women's Manifesto for Ghana, those who control land and its resources gain social and political power and authority; hence women's unequal land rights affect their access to other resources and their economic, social and political status. Nukunya in Awumbila (2001) also explains further that in patrilineal societies the women acquire land mainly through marriage and may lose it when the marriage ends. In places where the women can inherit, the portion allocated to daughters is often smaller than to that allocated to sons. Bukh (1979), Manuh (1990) and Benneh (1995) also add that ownership of land is restricted for many women, as they must rely on lineage and thus the *goodwill* of family heads who are invariably males. These gender-related problems have done much to hinder women farmers' agricultural progress, and, consequently, their economic progress.

The women's high desire to participate in any training program to upgrade themselves and their careers demonstrates that the women were determined to improve their level of economic empowerment. In a cross tabulation, Table 3 reveals that 94% of both the women with some formal education and those with no formal education desired to fully participate in any training program that was designed to upgrade or enhance their livelihoods. Such an attitude could promote a high and faster rate of economic empowerment among the women.

TABLE 3: THE LEVEL OF FORMAL EDUCATION IN RELATION TO THE WOMEN'S PARTICIPATION IN A TRAINING PROGRAM RELATIVE TO THEIR CAREERS

HIGHEST LEVEL OF FORMAL EDUCATION	The extent of participation in a training programme about your occupation in your community					
	Full		Casual		Total	
	Freg.	%	Freg.	%	Freq.	%
Primary School Level	16	8.8	1	0.6	17	9.3
J.S.S. Level	29	15.8	3	1.6	32	17.5
S.S.S. Level	36	19.7	5		36	19.7
Middle School Level	29	15.8	4	2.2	33	18
Training College	2	1.1	1	0.6	3	1.6
No formal education	57	31.1	2	1.1	60	32.8
No response	2	1.1			2	1.1
Total	171	93.5	11	6		

Source: Field Survey, 2001

From the results, it could be emphasized that generally the women had obtained a high level of economic independence. The table shows that almost 99% of the women were engaged in income-generating activities, 97% of them were able to manage their own income-generating activities; 63% were capable of controlling their own incomes; 83% were allowed by their husbands to cultivate for commercial purposes; 83% were allowed by their husbands to decide on how to use their own money; 88% of the women had access to land for their agricultural purposes, and 94% of them strongly desired to fully participate in any training program to upgrade themselves and their livelihoods. From these statistics, one can observe that the women had a high level of economic independence. Meanwhile, the women who found themselves at the most disadvantaged level, i.e., the 13.7% who totally depended on their husbands because they did not have any regular source of income, need to be given some capacity-building support so their level of dependence could be reduced.

In discussing economic activities among rural women, another crucial issue of consideration is housekeeping activities and its impact on the productivity of women. Time is seen as a very important resource and therefore how much progress these women could make on their jobs depends on effective and a more productive use of their time. The Ghana Living Standards Survey 4 (2000) shows that apart from time-use on economic activities, women use a lot of their time on housekeeping activities like fetching water, child care, sweeping, garbage disposal and cooking. Although these activities are part of everyday life, they usually take more of an individual's time and often at higher cost than is realised. From the national survey [GLSS 4, 2000] a breakdown of household activities shows that, on average, each person spends 35 minutes a day collecting wood, 38 minutes a day fetching water, 19 minutes sweeping, 11 minutes disposing garbage and about 3 hours taking care of children. An examination of the individual activities reveals that over a quarter of the population is engaged in wood collection and 4% spend at least an hour a day fetching wood. Collecting wood is done by a third (34.6%) of females of all ages, whereas less than a fifth of males engage in this activity. Among males, more of the younger ones, (ages 7-14 years), collect wood than the older ones. With the exception of Accra, the capital town of Ghana, wood fetching is common in all parts of the country.

In the case of water, 49% of the population obtain water without any loss of time, and about 38% spend an average of less than an hour a day fetching water; this still leaves 12% who have to spend an average of at least an hour every day fetching water. Rural dwellers spend more time fetching water (48 minutes on average per day) than their urban counterparts (37 minutes). The time spent on fetching water in the rural savannah is almost double the average for other rural areas and some urban communities.

As with fetching wood and water, the burden of other household chores falls mainly on females. The differences in the proportion of males and females involved in the other activities are more varied than fetching of wood and water. These differences are more pronounced with sweeping and cooking, where two-thirds of women are involved, although not more than a quarter of men are. Contrasting the urban and rural responses indicates that more time is spent on housekeeping in rural areas than urban areas, including almost all the activities except garbage disposal and wood fetching in Accra.

Table 4 shows time spent on housekeeping and domestic activities in Brong Ahafo Region of Ghana. Among people in that population ages 15 – 19, women and girls seem to engage more in fetching wood and water, childcare, sweeping, garbage disposal and cooking water than do men and boys.

TABLE 4: AVERAGE MINUTES PER DAY SPENT ON FETCHING WOOD, WATER, CHILD CARE, SWEEPING, GARBAGE DISPOSAL AND COOKING WATER BY AGE, AND SEX IN BRONG AHAFO REGION OF GHANA

Sex	Age group	Fetching Wood	Fetching Water	Child Care	Sweeping	Garbage Disposal	Cooking Water
M	7-14	29	39	33	24	22	51
	15-19	30	28	103	25	19	41
	20-24	27	19	-	11	10	34
	25-44	20	19	73	21	9	49
	45-59	19	26	38	25	17	50
	60 +	11	29	17	13	9	50
	All	26	31	60	22	20	47
F	7-14	33	35	93	28	20	62
	15-19	27	31	93	23	19	70
	20-24	32	40	195	27	14	89
	25-44	32	33	129	27	15	99
	45-59	35	35	79	25	14	83
	60 +	43	23	108	21	16	77
	All	33	34	122	26	17	85

Source: GLSS 4 (2000)

Therefore, to enhance productivity, it becomes crucial for governments and development practitioners to consider appropriate ways of facilitating these household activities, most especially among rural women. The use of appropriate, modern technology for provision of fuel or gas for cooking could be considered. Rural water projects and baby care facilities will have to be improved. Since the figures are high for both girls and women, such household activities could no doubt affect girl-child education in terms of available time for home studies and leisure. There will also be a need to sensitize both the youth and adults (through mass education), to raise awareness about the need to save time from housekeeping activities and invest more of their time in education and income-generation activities for higher productivity. The traditional notion of measuring standards in the ideal girl or woman (e.g., vigorous housekeeping work like good cooking, fetching, always keeping enough water in her pot and firewood in her kitchen, producing and nursing babies, and maintaining a good environment) will obviously have to be reconsidered as well. Thus, in addition to instilling these traditional standards and values in young women, they will have to be trained to give priority to the work necessary to achieve higher education and increase economic productivity.

Generally, it could be observed from the above discussion, that from observing the women of the Mo communities of Ghana and the Ghana Living Standards Survey 4 GLSS 4, 2000, rural women have low levels of formal educational attainment, and as a result, operate in the informal sector to make a living. However the issue of unemployment could not be highlighted among rural women. Though they might not be making higher income gains, in their own way, at their own level, the women are able to fend for themselves and manage their households from the small-scale jobs in which they engage. Meanwhile, housekeeping activities appear to affect rural women's productivity. Therefore, in addition to improving their level of formal educational attainment and income-generating activities, it will also be crucial to harness the potentials of appropriate technology for the purpose of easing the burden of housekeeping activities and thus provide the rural women more time and energy to invest in adult learning and income-generation activities. Recognizing the influence of the values traditional society places on woman's ability to work hard to manage the home, produce and nurse babies, it will be useful to awaken society to the need to promote economic independence among women and to place value on higher learning among girls and women in rural communities (Kwapong 2005).

PARTICIPATION IN DECISION-MAKING IN THE HOME

It is not only unequal access to land and control of other productive resources that constrains women but their absence at the decision-making table as well. It becomes more critical when women are not adequately represented on committees, boards and all fora for discussion of issues that affect them. The UN Secretary-General's report on *Economic Advancement for Women* (2006) indicates that recent global statistics show that women continue to increase their share of managerial positions but that the rate of progress is slow and uneven. Though the report observed that lack of comparable data remains a problem, there was little or no change and, in some, the percentage rates were even in decline. It is further remarked in the report that lack of access to decision-making positions was found both in professions dominated by men and in female-dominated sectors, where, despite the fact that more managers were women, a disproportionate number of men rose to the more senior positions.

Similarly, the Ghana Living Standard Survey 4 (GLSS, 2000) revealed that women in Ghana are poorly represented at all levels of decision-making, even though they represent 50.2% of the entire population. Within the household, culture and norms designate men as heads of households and therefore the principal decision-makers. At the highest level of government, women are again disadvantaged. Statistics show that women constitute 9.5% of the membership in Parliament and men 91%. At the bureaucratic level, women constitute 32% of the entire civil service, with 24% of them in local government performing secretarial and clerical responsibilities. Only 12% of the decision-influencing category, the administrative class, is female. A similar pattern is observed at the district level, where only 5% of elected representatives were women. Even though a government directive in 1998 reserved 30% of the appointed membership of assemblies for women, districts have used this figure as the maximum instead of a minimum, making the participation of women in top-level decision-making very low. Only 3 of the 110 Presiding Members are women; of the 110 district chief executives, 12 are women (10.9%). In the 2002 District Assembly elections, out of a total of 4,583 candidates elected, 341 (7.4%) were women, while 4,241 (92.5%) were men. Out of 7,700 members of the 110 District Assemblies, 38 (5%) are women. All the Metropolitan and Municipal Chief Executives are men (Ofei-Aboagye, E. 2000; Mensah – Kutin, 2003).

Meanwhile, as observed by Ofei-Aboagye (2000), lack of women's full participation in political decision-making has negative consequences for the society. It deprives women of important rights as well as responsibilities as citizens; it excludes their perspectives from policies and legislation; it prevents their input into national budgets and resource allocation and deprives society of women's skills, knowledge and their perspectives. With the dominance of tradition and culture in rural communities, coupled with the low levels of education among rural women, it becomes crucial to explore the situation of rural women in decision-making.

As explained by Oppong (1974), the process of decision-making in the home, how domestic tasks, responsibilities and resources should be allocated, is a complex sequence of events taking place between spouses and their kin. In most traditional Ghanaian communities, women do not take part in decision-making. However Benneh (1995) remarks that decision-making in the household is now believed to depend to a great extent upon the relative power position of the spouse. Both Benneh (1995) and Oppong (1974) share the view that contribution of resources for the upkeep of the household is an important factor in the decision-making process of the household. The educational level of the wife has also been considered as an important factor in household decision-making.

From the study it was realised that almost 79% of the Mo women had the option of sharing ideas with their spouses. Almost 75% of them said that they were able to express their views on the number of children to give birth to and the timing of those pregnancies. When asked to outline the types of decisions that they were able to make in their homes, 75.3% of the women could give concrete examples. The examples included decisions on meal planning and preparation, regulation of childbirth, family welfare, housekeeping and child-care. Only 26% of the women could not give examples. In relation to the women's level of involvement in the planning of the family's budget, the results showed that while 26.8% of the women reported to be highly involved, 43.2% were involved at an average level, with only 24% of the women being involved at a low level in the planning of their family's budget.

In responding to the extent to which they were allowed to decide on their own when planning to hand over their property to their heirs, 55% said they were able to do so to a high extent and 34.4% said that they were able to do that to a low extent. About 83% of the women also stated that they were allowed by their husbands to decide on how to use their income.

From the discussion so far, it could be deduced that the Mo Women under study had some level of participation in decision-making in the home, probably as a result of their level of economic independence. For instance, Ardayfio-Schandorf (1991), Benneh (1995) and Oppong (1974) explain that the contribution of resources for the upkeep of the home is an important factor in the decision-making process of the household. The wife's position in decision-making has weight when she has educational, occupational and financial resources and uses these in providing for the needs of the family. While the husband is the sole decision-maker, he will only consult his wife when he feels like it; in the event of financial difficulties on the part of the husband, the woman makes major decisions concerning the home. This brings to mind the expression by Greenstreet (1978) that the women's financial contribution to the family budget has enhanced her power position in the home, strengthening the woman's bargaining power.

Another significant observation that could be made from the results is that 97% of the women who were able to share ideas with their husbands to a *high extent* had their views taken; only 2.9% of them had their views rejected. For the women who were able to share ideas with their spouse to a *low extent*, only 44% of them had their views accepted, with the remaining 56% of the women having their views rejected (Table 1). This implies that, the higher one's ability of sharing ideas with one's spouse, the higher one's chances of having one's views accepted; conversely, the lower one's ability of sharing one's views with one's spouse, the lower one's chances of being listened to by one's husband In other words, the women who enjoyed a high level of sharing their views had a high level of influence in making decisions. It could therefore be emphasized that those at the high level of decision-making will be further motivated by having their views heard and considered. Additionally, one's economic achievement contributes to one's opportunity to be listened to as well.

TABLE 1: THE EXTENT OF ONE'S ABILITY TO SHARE IDEAS WITH THE SPOUSE IN RELATION TO ONE'S IDEAS BEING TAKEN IN GOOD FAITH

THE EXTENT OF ONE'S ABILITY TO SHARE IDEAS WITH THE SPOUSE	*ARE THE IDEAS TAKEN IN GOOD FAITH?*							
	Yes		No		No response	re-	T0tal	
	Fre q.	%	Freq .	%	Freq .	%	Freq .	%
Very high	49	26.8			-	-	49	26.8
High	52	28.4	3	1.6			55	30.1
Average	1	0.6	38	20	1.		39	21.3
Low	4	2.2	7	3.8			11	6
Very Low	7	3.8	7	3.8			14	7.6
No response	3	16.6			12	6.6	15	8.2
Total	116	63.4	55	30	13	7.1		

Source: Field Survey, 2001

However, there appeared to be some lapses in the women's decision- making capabilities, which need careful attention and intervention:

- From the results, we can see that almost 26% of the women could not report any decision that they were able to make in the home.
- On the women's level of involvement in the planning of the family's budget, almost 17% of the women said they were involved at a low level.
- 34.4% of the women said that their ability to decide on their own when planning to hand over their property to their heirs is at a low level.
- About 10% of the women said they were not allowed by their husbands to decide on how to use their own money.
- 9.3% of the women reported that although they were able to share ideas with their husbands, their views were not taken in good faith.

All these results show that some of the women lacked some decision-making abilities and therefore need some form of intervention or capacity-building to improve their decision-making skills. Experience in gender advocacy has revealed a need for male involvement in all efforts at empowering women. Husbands will have to be orientated to respect the views of their partners so that women will be able to build their confidence and express their views. It will help for husbands or men to consult wives or female colleagues often on family and other issues, rather than making solo decisions on their behalf. Giving women significant room to operate helps them to gain a high level of independence and confidence. Above all, cordiality among the family and community members will enhance each others morale. There is no doubt that women's recognition of gender inequality is important in enabling them to act to change not only their access to resources, but also their limited ability to participate in decision-making and to exercise autonomy in making decisions that affect them.

DECISION-MAKING IN THE COMMUNITY

The women's empowerment framework reflects the theoretical assumption that women's lives are constrained not only by unequal access to land and control of resources, but by their limited ability to participate in decision-making and to exercise autonomy in making decisions that affect them as well. The empowerment framework further assumes that the extent of women's own recognition of gender inequality is important in enabling them to act to change not only their access to resources but also to change their limited ability to participate in decision-making and to exercise autonomy in making decisions that affect them. It further assumes that the extent of women's own recognition of gender inequality is important in enabling them to act to change not only their access to resources but also to decision-making power. From the results of the survey, 71.6% of the women said they were allowed to express their views in public. The results also showed that when discussing issues of the community, 71.6% of the women recorded that they were invited by the elders to participate. This suggests that at least some of the women contribute to decision-making in the community. While 18% reported that they were invited very often, the large percentage of 56.3% reported to be invited only occasionally, with 24% reporting that they were never invited. It could be emphasized that although a high percentage of 71.6% indicated that they were allowed to express their views in public, the rate could be higher. However, one could probably say that depending on how one looks at it, many of the women had a chance of sharing their views in public.

As to whether the women's views were considered, 74.3% of the women said their views were valued, with 21.3% saying their views were not valued. This means that to a large extent, the women who had the opportunity to express their views in public had their views taken in good faith.

On the women's group affiliations, 66.1% said they had group affiliation, with 33.3% reporting to have no group affiliation. This shows that at least the women had some sort of affiliation, which could enhance their empowerment. As remarked by Rowlands (1993) and Karl (1995), the process of empowerment is both individual and collective. It is through involvement in groups that people most often begin to develop awareness and the ability to organize to take action and to bring about change. Rowlands and Karl continue, agreeing that by organizing themselves, and working collectively, women will be empowered to gain increased representation, which will lead to increased empowerment and ultimately greater control. When the women were questioned on the purpose of the women's associations, 27.9% said the associations gave occupational assistance; 19.1% said their work with associations was for welfare activities; 9.3% said their associations served religious purposes, and 35% of the women did not respond to the question because they had no group affiliation. But all 65% of the women who had group membership could mention the benefits that they derived from their associations, benefits which could have an impact and thus enhance their empowerment.

When the women's level of education was compared to their chances of being allowed to express their views in public, a critical observation of the results revealed that all the 21.3% of the women who had attained the highest level of education in the community, i.e., Secondary school and Training College, were able to express their views in public gatherings, while the 20.2% of the women who had never had the chance of expressing their views in public had attained low levels of education, like primary and Junior Secondary Schools, and no formal education at all. This result emphasizes that the level of education is a factor in one's ability to express oneself in public gatherings. Similarly, from Table 2 all the respondents (23.3%) with the highest level of education (SSS and Teacher Training College), with the exception of one (0.6%) respondent, reported that they had had the chance of being invited into the conversation by elders whenever they were discussing issues of the community. This observation further emphasizes that the level of education is a contributing factor in one's opportunity to contribute to decision-making in the community. As to whether their views were taken, all (1.6%) women who obtained a Teacher Training level responded in the affirmative, with only 0.5% of the Senior Secondary School (SSS) level, saying that her view was not taken, most likely because she did not have the chance at all. From these observations, we could deduce that the higher one's level of formal education the greater is one's ability to offer suggestions that are worth taking.

From the result on the women's participation in decision-making in the community, it becomes clear that increased attention has to be paid to inequalities in participation in decision-making, including persistent gender stereotypes which prevent women from having full participation in both public and private life. Pointing to the need to promote women's autonomy and participation in decision-making, the women's empowerment framework targets the possibility of changing social and political institutions in order to make such autonomy and participation possible. This is because, as noted by Tsikata (2001), societal arrangements make men control more resources, e.g., land, labour, capital (both monetary and social), than women, and men have the power to take important decisions as household heads, controllers of lineages, communities, work places and ultimately the state, thus practically all the power structures of the society.

TABLE 2: RELATIONSHIP BETWEEN LEVEL OF FORMAL EDUCATION AND INVITATION BY ELDERS WHEN DISCUSSING ISSUES OF THE COMMUNITY.

HIGHEST LEVEL OF FORMAL EDUCATION	*ELDERS INVITATION WHEN DISCUSSING ISSUES OF THE COMMUNITY*									
	Very often		Occasionally		Not at all		No response		Total	
	Freq.	%	Freq.	%	Freq.	%	Freq.	%	Freq.	%
Primary School Level	2	1.1	11	6	4	2.2			17	9.3
Middle School Level	11	6	15	8.2	7	3.8			33	18
J.S.S. Level	6	3.3	18	9.8	6	3.3	2	1.1	32	17.5
S.S.S. Level	4	2.2	13	16.9	1	0.6			36	19.7
Training College	1	0.6	2	1.1					3	1.6
No formal education	9	4.9	24	13.1	27	14.8			60	32.8
No response			2	1.1					2	1.1
Total	33	18	103	56.3	45	24.6	2	1.1		

Source: Field Survey, 2001

CONCLUSION

This discussion clearly reveals that the Mo women of Ghana's report a degree of participation in decision-making in both the home and the community. It could be observed that although the women had low levels of formal educational attainment, they had an appreciable level of participation in decision-making, which could probably be attributed to their level of economic independence. In view of this, it cannot be concluded that the influence of the women's low level of education had totally deprived them of participation in decision-making. Tsikata remarks that,

> There is no evidence that women who are not highly educated have not attained any level of empowerment, and therefore do not do well in public life. There have been examples of women in Ghanaian politics since the anti-colonial struggle who have used a little education to go very far, demonstrating that lack of education is not a bar to impressive performance in high office. (2001:59)

In any case, that the trends have changed, and the myth of men being the sole decision-makers is now being challenged, clearly echoes the views of Manu (1984) and Benneh (1995). The survey revealed that 71.6% of the women were allowed to express their views in public; 71.6% were invited by elders when discussing issues of the community; 74.3% of the women who were able to express their views had their views taken seriously; 66.1% belonged to women's associations; and 65% of the women were able to reference the benefits they derived from the associations.

Yet despite this result, there is need for improvement in order that the women who do not have the opportunity to express their views in public, that is the 24.6% who were not invited by elders when discussing issues of the community, the 21.3% whose views were not taken seriously, and the 33.3% of the women who did not belong to any association, in addition to the majority who had managed to gain some participation, could further improve their decision-making skills, and hopefully will be afforded the opportunity to do so in the future.

8
ADULT EDUCATION FOR EMPOWERMENT OF WOMEN OF MO

INTRODUCTION

The results obtained from the study of the women of Mo communities of Ghana offer several indications as to the use of adult education to empower women in rural communities. The focus of this study was to assess empowerment among the women of the Mo communities of the Brong-Ahafo Region of Ghana. Objectives were therefore set to find out how the bio-data of the respondents impacted on their empowerment; to observe the women's attainment in education; to identify the skills that the women had developed to be able to carry out their economic activities; to determine the level of the women's participation in decision-making in the home; and to measure the extent to which the women take part in decision-making in their communities. To achieve this, a sample of 200 women was used for the study. The instrument for the data collection was a structured questionnaire made up of 5 sections and 34 items. The items were a combination of closed and open-ended questions. The tool for the data analysis was percentages. The results were organized in tables. The data were collected in the local language from four Mo communities, Weila, New Longoro, Bamboi and Ayorya.

The study found that, regarding the background of the respondents, the majority of the women were within the active independent stage (ages 21-60 years), most had ended their formal education at the basic level; they were mainly affiliated to Christian and Islamic religions; the majority were married; and farming and trading were their most prominent occupations, i.e., they mainly operated in the informal sector to earn their livelihood.

The study also revealed that the women had a low level of educational attainment, an appreciable level of economic independence, and participated in decision-making in the home. Regarding decision-making in the community, the women had some level of participation. The study presents a challenge to Adult Educators and other change agents to undertake capacity-building activities to improve the women's level of empowerment. The results have been presented in detail below, showing the implications of the study for adult education.

SUMMARY OF FINDINGS

Personal Characteristics

The great majority of the subjects (94%) fell within the active years of 21-60. They were in their independent adulthood stage of development, and, for that matter, formed the labour force of the entire community. Generally, the respondents had a low level of formal education, with 33.9% of the women being illiterate and 44.8% attaining schooling up to only the basic level (Middle, Primary, and Junior Secondary Schools). Almost all the respondents had religious affiliation. The majority were Christians, followed by Moslems and Traditional Religious believers. 77% of the women were married, with only 13.7 being single. With 71% of the women being farmers, and 68.3% indicating trading as their non-farming income-generating activity, farming and trading emerged as the major occupations in the area. The most encouraging aspect of the women's occupation was that the issue of unemployment was not prevalent among them. Almost all of the women reported that they were engaged in some form of income-generating activity, be it farming or petty trading.

Educational Attainment

From the study it was observed that the women had a low level of formal education. About 32.8% of the women had no formal education, 44.89% schooled up to the basic level, and 1.16% had attended training college. Meanwhile, about 97% of the women indicated their desire to participate in training programmes to upgrade themselves and their careers, which implies that the women were determined to enhance themselves. At the same time, 94% reported that they were eager to promote female education.

Economic Engagements

The results of the study revealed that almost 99% of the women engaged in income-generating activities. Of that 99%, 97% reported to be able to manage their own income-generating activities; 83% were allowed by husbands to decide on how to use their own money; 88% of the women had access to land for agricultural purposes; 83% were allowed by their husbands to cultivate for commercial purposes; 63% were capable of controlling or managing their own income; and 94% of the women were strongly determined to partake in any training programme to upgrade themselves and improve upon their career. Based on these results, it could be emphasized that the women had a high level of economic independence. Further analysis revealed that 64% of the women depended on their husbands because they did not have a regular source of income. This implies that the women need to be strengthened or assisted in order to reduce their level of dependence and enhance their level of independence.

Participation in Decision-Making in the Home

From the analysis it was found out that as many as 79% of the women studied were able to share ideas with their spouse; 75% said they were able to express their views on family planning; 75% could give examples of the types of decisions they were able to make in the home; 94% were involved in the planning of their family's budget; 90% were able to decide on their own to hand over their properties to their heirs; 83% were allowed by their husbands to decide on how to use their money; and 97% of the women who were able to share ideas with their spouses had their views accepted. These results reaffirm that the women had high participation in decision-making in the home. There were however, a few lapses which would require capacity-building to improve upon their situation.

Participation in Decision-Making in the Community

The study showed that 71.6% of the women indicated that they were allowed to express their views in public; 71.6% of the women reported to be invited by elders when discussing issues of the community; 74.3% of the women who had the chance of expressing their views reported to have had their views accepted; and 66.1% of the women belonged to women's associations, with 65% being able to mention the benefits that they derived from the associations. Based on these results, it could be observed that the women had a relatively high level of participation in decision-making in the community. However, there is the need for improvement to further empower both the women who had the chance of participating in decision-making and the few who seemed not to be involved in decision-making at all.

On a general note, the women's level of educational attainment, economic independence, and participation in decision-making could no doubt contribute to their empowerment. However, considering that empowerment is a broad concept, there could be a limitation in the study because it was limited to only the education, economic and decision-making aspects of women's empowerment. But then the results present a challenge to Adult Educators and other change agents to undertake and intensify capacity-building and human development activities to improve the women's level of empowerment in all aspects. Furthermore, when considering the status of women, Ghana's Vision 2020, which targets gender inequality or human resource development among its principal objectives, lists human resource capacity-building as a focus for development assistance.

ADULT EDUCATION FOR EMPOWERMENT OF RURAL WOMEN

It can be noted from the findings of the study that the women under study had generally obtained some level of educational attainment, economic independence, and participation in decision-making, which could contribute to their empowerment. Nevertheless, there is still room for improvement in the areas of educational attainment, economic independence, and participation in decision-making in the home and the community. The women need capacity building so that their level of empowerment can be enhanced. One may even remark that since empowerment is a broad concept, focus will have to be extended to all the other areas of women's empowerment as well. As observed in the UN Report of the Secretary General on Women (2006), increased attention must be paid to inequalities in participation in economic decision-making, including persistent gender stereotypes that prevent women making progress in public life. Additionally, understanding the employment situations of and opportunities for rural women requires further research, strengthened data-collection efforts, and appropriate interventions.

To achieve this, Adult Education becomes an essential tool, as education has been identified as the foremost agent of empowerment. As Pomary expresses it,

> No matter how we run away from it, the foremost agent of empowerment is education: education is the only passport to liberation, to political and financial empowerment. Education contributes to sustainable development. It brings about a positive change in our lifestyles. It has the benefit of increasing earnings, improving health and raising productivity. (1992:21)

Adult education has a crucial role in achieving this. It has been internationally observed that adult and lifelong learning are deeply linked to social, economic and political justice; equality of gender relations; the universal right to learn; living in harmony with the environment; respect for human rights; recognition of cultural diversity; peace; and the active involvement of women and men in decisions affecting their lives. Adult Education has tremendous potential for development of the human capital and society at large. The need to use adult education for human resource development has been broadly highlighted in the various reports of the International Conferences of Adult Education (ICAE). In the most recently held ICAE (2004), which focused on adult education for poverty reduction, it was observed that 70% of the world's poor are women. To compensate for earlier educational inadequacies and empower people with the necessary knowledge, understanding and skills for sustainable participation in a constantly changing world, adult education at all levels is an unconditional essential.

At the 1997 Conference at Hamburg, it was emphasised that the informed and effective participation of men and women in every sphere of life is needed if humanity is to survive and to meet the challenges of the future. Recognising this, adult education was seen as more than a right and a key to the twenty-first century. Adult education is both a consequence of active citizenship and a condition for full participation in society. It is a powerful concept for fostering ecologically sustainable development, for promoting democracy, justice, gender equity, and scientific, social and economic development, and for building a world in which violent conflict is replaced by dialogue and a culture of peace based on justice. Adult learning can shape identity and give meaning to life. The Conference recognized that women have a right to equal opportunities; society, in turn, depends on their full contribution in all fields of work and aspects of life. It was therefore proposed that youth and adult learning policies should be responsive to local cultures and give priority to expanding educational opportunities for all women, while respecting their diversity and eliminating prejudices and stereotypes that both limit their access to youth and adult education and restrict the benefits they derive from them. The Conference emphasized that any attempts to restrict women's right to literacy, education and training must therefore be considered unacceptable. Indeed, practices and measures should be taken to counter them.

In its three-year Agenda for the Future 2003 – 2003, ICAE again enforced the use of adult education for the promotion of gender equality and women's empowerment. Under its fourth theme on *Adult Learning, Gender Equality and Equity, and the Empowerment of Women*, the Agenda outlines strategies for the promotion of women's empowerment through adult education. The Agenda observes that equal opportunity in all aspects of education is essential to enable women of all ages to make their full contribution to society and to discover the resolution of the multiple problems confronting humanity. When women are caught in a situation of social isolation and lack of access to knowledge and information, they are alienated from decision-making processes within the family, community and society in general, and they have little control over their bodies and lives. For poor women, the sheer business of survival becomes an obstacle to education. Educational processes should therefore address the constraints that prevent women's access to intellectual resources and empower women to become fully active as partners in social transformation. The message of equality and equal access must not be limited to programmes intended for women. Education should ensure that women become aware of the need to organize as women in order to change the situation and build their capacities, so that they can gain access to formal power structures and decision-making processes in both private and public spheres. This makes adult education crucial in the women's empowerment process.

Analysis of the study among the women of the Mo communities revealed that 32.8% of the women had no formal education at all, and 44.8% completed their formal education at the basic level (Primary, Junior Secondary and Middle School). Only 1.6% had completed Teacher Training education, and 17.5% had achieved schooling to the secondary level. As a result of their low level of education, the women engaged in small-scale businesses in the informal sector, undertaking such activities as farming, petty-trading, brewing of local drinks and shea butter extraction, among others, to earn income for survival. Only 3.3% of the women were in the Civil/public service sector. Due to the inconsistent and low-profit making nature of their jobs, 56.3% of the women did not have a regular source of income. To some extent the women's low level of education had also affected their chances of sharing their views in public and having their views accepted.

This implies that, as observed by Adult Educators world wide, the women need skills-training to improve upon their income-generating activities, literacy programs to upgrade their reading and writing skills, awareness-creation programs in general, and access to public information to make them more enlightened. With this sort of capacity- building and human development activities, coupled with some incentives for higher productivity, the women's capacity could be enhanced. Specific adult educational activities for the different areas of study to facilitate the women's empowerment process could include the following:

Education: Noting that 32.8% of the women studied had no formal education at all, it becomes crucial to promote female education. The female youth of the community could be counselled, encouraged and given the necessary assistance to be able to go through formal education to a higher level, to the extent that they will become well-equipped to operate in higher competitive productive activities. Similarly, functional literacy programmes for the female adults will help improve their reading and writing skills. Obviously such skills will further enhance the women's access to public and educational information.

Adult educators, development workers and other change agents will have to ensure that policies and practices comply with the principle of equitable representation of both sexes, especially at the managerial and decision-making levels of educational programs. Women and men will also have to be educated to acknowledge the serious and adverse impacts of globalization and structural adjustment policies in all parts of the world, especially upon women.

To widen access and enhance effectiveness in the promotion of female youth and adult education, there will be the need to remove barriers to access to formal and non-formal education, in particular in the case of pregnant adolescents and young mothers. Gender-sensitive participatory pedagogy, which acknowledges the daily life experience of women and recognizes both cognitive and affective outcomes, will also have to be promoted. Another strategy will be taking adequate legislative, financial and economic measures and implementing social policies to ensure women's successful participation in adult education through the removal of obstacles and the provision of supportive learning environments. Recognising that the burden of housekeeping roles affects women's productive and study time, educating women and men in such a way as to promote the sharing of multiple workloads and responsibilities will be of great help.

The use of information technology like radio, internet, and handheld devices will help reach the women and youth in remote areas. Studies have shown that women are willing to pay for such services (Kwapong 2005).

Economic Empowerment: To achieve or promote economic empowerment among women, it will be crucial for change and development agents to organise training for them in farming and other small scale businesses, so that they will be able to be able to acquire more skills to enhance their career options.

Traditional authorities could also manage to remove the traditional inhibitions which prevent women from getting equal access to land for agricultural purposes.

Incentives like credit facilities, modern technology for higher productivity, extension services and other assistance will have to be made available to women so that they can improve upon their production and be able to acquire sufficient capital and a regular source of income as well.

In addition, women will have to be encouraged and educated to engage in banking transactions other than the 'susu' (saving money with unauthorized individuals) means of saving money, so that they could benefit from incentives like loans from banks. If women are not comfortable with the bank's formalities, the banks will have to be brought to the level of the women.

Decision-Making in the Home: As much as is possible, it will be useful to focus family life education on encouraging communication among couples. Gender advocates have seen the need for male involvement in all efforts at empowering women. Husbands and all males will have to be counselled and socialized to respect the views of their partners, so that women will be able to build their confidence and express their views. In family and business issues, rather than making decisions on their behalf, it would be helpful for husbands to often consult their wives and for men to consult their female colleagues. Giving women latitude to operate would help them to gain a higher level of independence and confidence. Above all, cordiality among the family and community members will enhance each other's morale and facilitate the entire process.

Another strategy would combat domestic and sexual violence by providing appropriate education for men and supplying information and counselling to increase women's ability to protect themselves from such violence.

Decision-Making in the Community: Recognizing the influence of men in society and on women, opinion-leaders, who are mostly men, could be informed to encourage or motivate more women to express their views in public so that they too could contribute to the development of their communities. Thus women's participation in decision-making processes and in formal structures will have to be encouraged.

As much as possible, in addition to the queen-mother position, women could be given key positions among the elders in the traditional, political and other decision-making institutions. In this case it will be helpful to equip women with leadership skills for effective participation in all levels of decision-making and governance in their various communities.

If they are to bring about change, women will have to be encouraged to organize and create women's organizations in order to promote a collective identity.

Various religious organizations could also encourage women to become involved in leadership positions of the religious associations and other interest groups that undertake educational activities to facilitate their processes of empowerment.

CONCLUSION

The objective of adult education is to improve the situation of people by increasing their skills, knowledge and sensitivity. The survey on the women of Mo communities of Ghana helped to assess the women's educational, economic and decision-making levels. The study revealed that the women had attained some level of formal education and economic independence, and an appreciable level of participation in decision-making in the home and the community. Meanwhile, about 32.8% of the women had no formal education at all: 44.8% completed their formal education at the basic level (Primary, JSS and Middle School); only 1.6% had completed the Teacher Training education, and 17.5% schooled up to the secondary school level. As a result of their low level of education, the women engaged in small-scale private businesses like farming, petty-trading, brewing, shea-butter extraction, etc., to earn income for survival, with only 3.3% of the women working in the formal sector. Due to their dominance in the informal sector and the inconsistent nature of their jobs, 56.3% of the women did not have a regular source of income. Adult educational programs are crucial to enhance the women's capabilities; to help them organize themselves; to improve their skills for generating income; to increase their self-reliance; to assert their independent right to make decisions or choices, and to gain control over resources, all of which will assist them in challenging and eliminating their subordinate position in society.

9
STUDIES AND CASES OF ICT'S AND ADULT EDUCATION FOR WOMEN'S EMPOWERMENT

INTRODUCTION

There exists an extensive and diverse literature on the potential role of ICT in poverty alleviation, and, more specifically, on rural adult education in Sub-Sahara Africa and other developing areas. The literature cuts across disciplines, methodologies, theories and motivations. A comprehensive computer-based search of the literature on adult education in rural areas suggested that it may be useful to organize the sections of the literature along three main strands: 1) review of qualitative studies; 2) review of the theoretical and empirical literature and 3) case studies of the application of specific ICT protocols. This literature survey serves several important purposes. First, it is intended to help identify the critical factors influencing the use of ICT in rural adult education. These factors are then used in designing a survey instrument to be administered in selected areas in rural Ghana. The literature search also helps in identifying methodologies and approaches that have been applied in studying this subject matter; and, finally, the survey information provides a basis for a comparative assessment of households' responses to similar resource constraints.

QUALITATIVE STUDIES

Things that are being referred to as 'qualitative studies' consists of policy documents from domestic sources, international conferences and meetings, speeches, presentations, and private research initiatives. These studies have generally contributed to 1) defining the concept of ICT use in rural adult education, and 2) understanding the factors influencing ICT use in rural adult education.

ICT'S AND ADULT EDUCATION FOR WOMEN'S EMPOWERMENT

Ghana: ICT for Accelerated Development Policy (ICT4D), a publication released by the Government of Ghana in 2003, is the basic document outlining Ghana's vision for exploiting the massive potential of modern information and communication technologies. (http://www.ict.gov.gh/pdf/ DA: 12/18/04). According to the policy document, the *ultimate objective* is to "accelerate Ghana's socio-economic development process towards the realization of the vision to transform Ghana into a high income economy and society that is predominantly information-rich and knowledge-based within the next two to three decades or less" (14). The policy document defined the key priority areas of policy focus -- the "14 ICT4AD Pillars." The policy document sets the tone for the issues addressed in this thesis because it explicitly points to a need to use ICT to "bridge the gender gap" in Ghana.

The objective to utilize ICT to bridge the gender gap ties very well to the long-standing societal objective to promote adult education. A comprehensive definition of adult education, suggested by the United Nations Educational Scientific and Cultural Organization (UNESCO) about thirty years ago, supports the need for widespread use of ICT in adult education:

> The term adult education denotes the entire body of organized educational processes, whatever the content, level and method, whether formal or otherwise, whether they prolong or replace initial education in schools, colleges and universities, as well as apprenticeship, whereby persons regarded as adults by the society to which they belong develop their abilities, enrich their knowledge, improve their technical or professional qualifications or turn them into a new direction and bring about changes in their attitudes of behaviour in two-fold perspective of full personal development and participation in balanced and independent social, economic and cultural development. (UNESCO 1976)

The 1976 conference advocated innovative teaching methods such as remote teaching programmes, including correspondence courses, radio and television, to encourage the broadest possible participation in locally-based adult education.

The conference was especially mindful of the special needs of women, given the high incidence of illiteracy among this group. In earlier conferences (1960 and 1972), UNESCO had emphasized the use of science and technology (film, radio and television) in adult education, and the need for adult learners at the grass-roots level to participate in the planning, management and realization of their own affairs. The conference also raised the issue of public versus private participation in rural adult education. While the conference seemed to suggest an emphasis on the public role, recent economic and political realities seem to suggest a shift towards more private and commercial participation in the process.

Private researchers have also examined the relationship between ICT and adult education. In defining ICT for development, Rebecca Holmes (2004) adopted the Association for Progressive Communications definition of ICT as:

Technologies and tools that people use to share, distribute, gather information, and to communicate with one another, one on one, or in groups, through the use of computers and interconnected computer networks. They are mediums that utilize both telecommunication and computer technologies to transmit information. (24)

Holmes (2004) makes several important observations. For example, the author emphasizes the fact that ICTs are tools that facilitate sharing information and foster communication. Also, ICTs include both new and traditional information and communication technologies, and even though there is often an emphasis on the new, i.e., personal computers, the Internet, World Wide Web, mobile phones, satellite and wireless technologies, an African ICT tool kit for development also encompasses traditional media, including telephone, radio, television, print media (for example: newsletters, cartoons and graphic posters, and community communication initiatives (for example, listening groups and community theatre).

The donor literature has also attempted to identify critical factors influencing ICT use in adult education in rural areas. A typical example is the observation in the *Strategic Plan* of ICAE, the International Council of Adult Education (2003-2006), to the effect that the critical importance of adult education in economic development has been recognized in several important documents, including the Universal Declaration of Human Rights in 1948, the Declaration of the International Conference on Adult Education in Hamburg in 1997, and the World Forum on Education for All in Dakar in 2000.

These declarations and documents emphasize the international consensus that has been reached on the right to education and the right to learn throughout life for women and men, as well as on the central role of adult education in support of creative and democratic citizenship. The Hamburg Declaration focused specifically on the importance of participation of both sexes in the very existence of mankind: "The informed and effective participation of men and women in every sphere of life is needed if humanity is to survive and meet the challenges of the future." The strategy paper specifically points out "the potential of enabling creative and democratic citizenship, giving a voice to people living in poverty, as well as tools for improving their lives" through the application of ICT in adult education.

ICAE followed up the 1997Conference on Adult Education in Hamburg, with a study, *Agenda for the Future – Six Years Later*. On the issue of gender, the document pointed to several gaps in the effort to extend literacy to rural women. There was still a very high disparity in the literacy rate between men and women, and, more importantly, several countries do not have programs focusing on women and their participation in making decisions about such important issues as active citizenship and re-productive and sexual health. The report called for the empowerment of women to participate in decision-making on these important issues (ICAE Report 2003, http://www.icae.org.uy/ DA: 11/27/04).

In January, 2002, (UN, 2002a), the nations of the world reaffirmed their commitment to the use of technology in adult education when the United Nations General Assembly proclaimed the years 2003-2012 to be the UN Literacy Decade. The final UN resolution (56/116) reaffirmed the Dakar Framework for Action (UNESCO 2000a), in which the commitment was made to achieve a 50% improvement in adult literacy by 2015, especially for women, and to achieve equitable access to basic and continuing education for all adults. The International Action Plan for implementing Resolution 56/166 states that "Literacy for all is at the heart of basic education for all, and creating literate environments and societies is essential for achieving goals of eradicating poverty, reducing child mortality, curbing population growth, achieving gender equality and ensuring sustainable development, peace and democracy" (UN, 2002b,3). It is noteworthy that policy makers around the world recognize the need for adult education, not as an end in itself but rather as a means for making true improvements in the lives of people, for the realization of a peaceful and democratic world.

The Food and Agricultural Organization (FAO) has echoed the above sentiments. In his opening address, Wariboko Q-B West, FAO Representative to the Republic of South Africa, remarked that in the rural areas where most of the world's poor live, women are major producers in the local economies. ICT's can be used as tools to empower rural women with the technological information and skills necessary for sustainable food security and livelihood. New information and communication technologies hold a unique opportunity for women in the developing world to speak out, to be more visible and less isolated, and hence to support their increased political, social and economic participation at every level. He added that FAO takes a multi-technology approach to the application of ICT's. This approach promotes the role of traditional and modern communication technologies (linking up rural radios with multi-purpose development centres, promoting distance education for rural populations, especially women, database management for food security, agriculture education, and extension work). The FAO actively promotes community radio as well as IT-based interactive learning (http://www.fao.org/sd/ruralradio/en/index.html, DA: 11/12/04).

RURAL POVERTY, STATUS OF RURAL WOMEN, AND ICT IN GHANA

The basic document summarizing the state of poverty in Ghana is the "Ghana Poverty Reduction Strategy," a paper from 2003. The GPRS defines poverty as "unacceptable physiological and social deprivation."(3) and lists participation in decision-making, health, education, environmental sustainability, and lack of political power as some of the critical considerations in defining poverty (GPRSP, 2003). Figure 4. 1 Shows the incidence of poverty in the ten regions in Ghana.

Figure 4.1. Regional Distribution of Poverty in Ghana

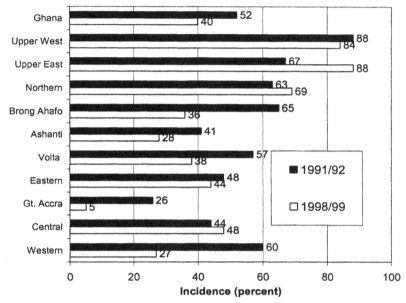

Source: GPRS, 2003

According to the GPRS, five out of ten regions had more than 40% of their population living in poverty in 1999. The three northern regions (Upper East, Upper West and Northern Regions) are the hardest hit with nine out of ten people in the Upper East, eight out of ten people in the Upper West, and seven out of ten people in the Northern Regions classified as poor in 1999 (GPRS 2003, ii). Ghana has experienced some success in reducing poverty, as "overall poverty decreased between 1991/92 and 1998/99 from 51.7% to 39.5%. Extreme poverty declined from 36.5% to 26.8% over the same period. However, unchecked population growth threatens potential gains in poverty reduction since population growth during the decade of the Nineties far outstripped the rate of decline in poverty levels (GPRS, 17).

The high incidence of poverty among women presents a major barrier to ICT adoption. The GLSS 4 (2000) survey concluded, "Women form over 70% of food crop farmers, and 90% of those in internal agricultural distribution, marketing and processing. About 80% of Ghanaian women in the labour force are employed in small, semi-formal and informal undertakings "(Figure 4. 2).

There are other constraints which could limit the employment of ICT in empowering rural women. In Ghana, of the adult illiterate population (those 15 years of age who cannot read and write at least a sentence), women constitute the higher percentage (42%). Studies have shown that women experience greater poverty, have heavier time burdens, lower rates of utilization of productive resources, and lower literacy rates (GLSS 4). School participation rates for basic

Figure 4. 2: Poverty among Socio – Economic Groups in Ghana

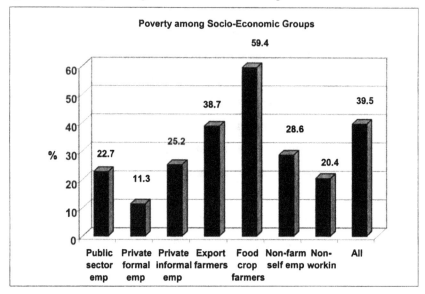

Source: Ghana Statistical Service, 2000, Poverty Trends in the 1990s, Accra

and second cycle schools are 77% for men and 38% for women. This discrepancy widens as one ascends the educational ladder (Republic of Ghana 1995:6; Ghana - Vision 2020: The First Step, 1996-2000).

Prospects for a change in the near future are not bright, given the record of current recruitment into the literate class. Gross primary one admission and primary school enrollment ratios have not significantly improved since 1992. Dropout rates remain high at about 20% for boys and 30% for girls at Primary School, and 15% for boys and 30% for girls at Junior Secondary School. Programs targeting empowerment of rural women through ICT applications must take into account the targeted population designated to use the technology."

There are also major barriers to introducing ICT to rural women due to the political context within which rural women function in Ghana. In a true sense, the idea of *empowerment* is captured / defined by the participation of rural women in all phases of policies and programs that affect them, i.e., design, implementation, and evaluation. The literature is replete with calls for "stakeholder ownership" of development policies and programs to ensure success. Unfortunately, the participation of women in decision-making is the weakest link in the fight against poverty. The GLSS 4 concluded that women are poorly represented at all levels of decision-making. Within the household, culture and norms designated men as heads of households and therefore the principal decision-makers.

At the highest level of government, women are again disadvantaged. Women constitute 9.5% of the membership in Parliament, while men constitute 91%. At the bureaucratic level, women constitute 32% of the entire civil service, with 24% of those in local government performing secretarial and clerical responsibilities. Only 12% of the decision-influencing category – the administrative class – is female.

A similar pattern is observed at the district level, where only 5% of elected representatives were women. Even though a government directive in 1998 reserved 30% of the appointed membership of assemblies for women, districts have used this figure as the maximum instead of a minimum, making the participation of women in top-level decision-making very low. The level of participation by women excludes their perspectives from policies and legislation; it prevents their input into national budgets and resource allocation; and it deprives society of women's skills, knowledge, and perspectives (Ofei-Aboagye 2000; Doyphyne 2000). The conclusion that emerges from this brief background of the poverty situation in Ghana is that policies and programs to promote ICT in empowering women in rural areas have to be undertaken with due consideration of the broader socio-economic environment within which women function in Ghana.

ICT ENVIRONMENT IN GHANA

Another consideration is the availability of complementary inputs such as computers, voice and video systems, and, in some cases, physical access to rural locations. The current infrastructure for telecommunication broadcasts to regions in Ghana is limited to serving the major regional centres, capitals and urban areas (Figure 4.3). Resources for expanding the reach of the telecommunication infrastructure may be quite limited in light of the findings of a recent survey of budget allocations to the ICT sector. According to the report (Table 4), "the majority of government ministries and public sector organizations have less than 10% of their total budget allocated for ICT (including acquisition of hardware, software, training, maintenance of ICT systems, etc.). Close to 60% indicated that their ICT expenditure (as a percentage of their total expenditure) is below 10%. Close to 34% of the organizations reported devoting about a quarter of their total expenditure on ICT's. On the whole, most of the organizations in all the sectors spend less than half of their annual budget on ICT (2003 National ICT Policy and Plan Development Committee, Republic of Ghana 2004: http://www.ict.gov.gh, DA 02/19/2005).

The other complementary products to enhance the use of ICT resources in rural areas are difficult to obtain and very expensive even if made available. Sometimes the availability of these resources is beyond the control of the rural dweller. A good example is electricity. According to the GPRS, the percentage of the rural population with access to electricity rose from 8.7% in 1992 to 17.6%

Table 4. 1. Survey Results of Expenditures on ICT by Government Ministries

Percentage distribution of IT expenditure as per percentage of total organizational expenditure	All Sectors	Government Ministries	Public Sector Organizations
0%(none)	4%	8%	0%
Below 10%	60%	71%	48%
About 25%	34%	21%	48%
About 50%	2%	0%	4%
About 75%	0%	0%	0%
About 100%	0%	0%	0%

Source: National ICT Policy and Plan Development Committee, 2003

in 1999. The GPRS projection is to increase the number of households with access to electricity for domestic, commercial and industrial uses to 20% by 2004 (2003:3, 64). Ownership of ICT-related technology and equipment is also very limited in rural areas. The GLSS showed the radio player to be the most-owned information technology, as reported by 34% of respondents, followed by radio, which was owned or used by 14% of respondents. Record players and video decks emerged as the least owned, by 1.2% and 1.4% respondents respectively. Only about 11% of the rural people owned television sets, probably due to the absence of electricity in many rural areas (Table 4. 2). While these constraints provide a rationale for considering technologies like handheld devices that do not require an elaborate infrastructure for support, it must be borne in mind that these technologies are expensive and may require considerable training to successfully introduce to rural communities with little formal education and knowledge of modern technology. Such daunting problems call for the need to engage in a study that could provide needed information to guide policymaking, program planning and implementation of ICTs and adult education for empowerment of women in rural areas in Ghana.

Table 4.2 Proportion of households owning various assets and consumer durables by locality (percent)

Asset/ consumer durable	Urban			Rural				%	National estimates	
	Accra	Other urban	All	Coastal	Forest	Savannah	All		Households owning	Total owned
				(Percentages)				(millions)		
Radio	9.8	13.9	12.8	12.5	15.7	13.0	14.2	13.7	0.56	0.59
Radio cassette	58.4	48.0	51.0	29.8	37.8	30.1	34.0	40.2	1.64	1.78
Record player	3.9	3.8	3.8	0.8	1.8	0.3	1.2	2.1	0.09	0.09
3-in-1 Radio	10.0	5.5	6.8	1.0	2.4	0.2	1.5	3.4	0.14	0.15
Video	12.3	5.8	7.6	1.7	1.9	0.3	1.4	3.9	0.16	0.16
Television	48.2	36.1	39.5	13.2	14.0	2.5	10.9	21.4	0.87	0.94
Sample size	620	1579	2199	899	1940	960	3799	5998	(13.43)	

Source: GLSS 4.

THEORETICAL AND EMPIRICAL STUDIES

Theoretical Literature

There are not many formal models of the interface between ICT and rural adult education. Rather, researchers have focused on the formal relationship between technology, education and poverty-alleviation generally. One particular study is that of Rebecca Holmes (2004). Holmes presents a rich framework for understanding ICT and rural development. Even though Holmes' framework focuses on the role of ICT on a specific sector (governance of the economy), it still offers valuable insights in the understanding of how good governance and the various strategic actors and their roles influence and are influenced by women's empowerment in other contexts. One such context is rural women's empowerment through ICT. The table points to the comprehensiveness and complexity of the empowerment problem, given the many stakeholder interests that must be reconciled to achieve an efficient policy outcome. The table also indicates that empowerment may entail the expenditure of considerable human and financial resources. For example, what the author refers to as "gender budgeting" ensures that resources available serve the needs of all women, especially rural women.

A second example which illustrates the need for human and financial resources is the need to have the relevant information to guide policy making. Holmes' framework emphasizes the need to collect gender and location (urban/slum/per-urban/rural) desegregated data to evaluate government policy and develop new policies that support the empowerment of women. One important conclusion from Holmes' framework is the extent of resources needed to develop programs to empower women through the use of ICT. It is in this context that a study of sustainable ICT-use in rural empowerment must pay some attention to the sources of funding to implement programs.

Vikas Nath (2001) has presented a formal model of the role of ICT in empowerment of women. The author explains that "ICT in the context of knowledge societies is understood as building the ability and skills of women to gain insight of actions and issues in the external environment which influence them and to build their capacity to get involved and voice their concerns in these external processes, and make informed decisions." The author adds that this entails building the capacities of women to overcome social and institutional barriers, and strengthening their participation in the economic and political processes to improve the quality of their lives (http://www.cddc.vt.edu/knownet/articles / womenand ICT.htm DA: 11/27/2004).

Nath's (2001) model implies that women's access to strategic information leads to their empowerment. Though the model is cognizant of the various conceptualization processes that information goes through in the women's system, it does not take into consideration various inhibiting factors and obstacles that could affect the women's empowerment. For example, the model does not advance the scholar in his/her search as to how the socio-political milieu could affect the availability of information. Also, given the set of hierarchical cultural structures within which rural women function, the implicit assumption that access to strategic information automatically empowers a rural household is suspect, which means women's access to strategic information does not lead to automatic empowerment. Furthermore, there is no indication of how the needed information is to be acquired and who is to pay for it. Nath's model does not indicate a feedback loop, so that access to information is seen as a unidirectional process. The essence of empowerment is the ability to use information in making choices that supposedly would influence future participation in policy choice, with decisions being made to alleviate poverty. Despite these observations about the model, it must be pointed out that Nath is one of few authors to rigorously define the theoretical underpinnings of ICT and rural adult education. In this sense, the author provides an opportunity to identify and specify hypotheses that would be tested using field data from selected rural areas in Ghana.

EMPIRICAL STUDIES - COSTING ICTS IN ADULT EDUCATION

There are two strands of the empirical literature relevant to this discussion. First, there is the literature that examines the cost of establishing ICT systems in different cultural contexts, and second there is the literature that summarizes the impacts of introducing identifiable ICT interventions on rural households, e.g., the effect of age, gender, income, and educational level on a households' choice of ICT. An example of the first strand of empirical literature is the study by Perraton (2000). The author provides some data on the cost of some adult basic education projects from several countries to show the economic advantage that distance education has over face-to-face. One is likely to break even fiscally, if the product is highly accessed. In any case, the type of media is also a factor. For instance, Perraton (2000) explains that studies have revealed that radio offers a moderate cost for distance programmes for adults in health and agriculture. Radio has a large audience, a moderate cost of production, and a delivery leading to a lower cost per learner. According to Haddad & Jurich (2002) as quoted by Wagner et al (2003), to make a realistic cost estimates one needs to take into account the equation:

$$TC = FC + VC [N]$$

where, **TC** is the *Total Cost*, N is the *Number of Learners Served*; **FC** is the *Fixed Costs,* such as minimum infrastructure (e.g., Internet basics); and **VC** is the *Variable Costs* or 'recurrent costs,' such as training costs related to the numbers of participants-- learners, teachers, etc.

What may be generally emphasized is that cost-effectiveness can be influenced greatly (and positively) by the 'reach' of a given ICT solution, especially if fixed costs can be controlled. Thus Interactive Radio Instruction (IRI) has one of the lowest rates of unit costs (between 1-3 dollars/learner), as the denominator in many countries goes into the hundreds of thousands of individual learners. Considering cost-effectiveness only by the above equation necessarily ignores the parameter (and critical issue) of learning achievement. Further, reaching adult learners provides relatively little information on whether individual lives are improved. What is missing from most of these cost analyses is a consideration of learning effectiveness. Wagner et al, (2003) expresses that even though this study is one of the best recent ICT evaluation studies on World's work in Africa, relatively little direct data was obtained on actual learner achievement and none on costs incurred.

Wagner et al. (2003) adds that, with respect to ICT, not only must important policy choices be made, but choices must be made in a very timely fashion, if they are not to be devalued due to obsolescence.

These factors must be borne in mind by any decision-maker who is contemplating purchases of ICT for education. The contrasting choices that must be dealt with simultaneously are most crucial, confirming that it is not very easy to accomplish rationally. It is no surprise that ICT has become one of the most difficult decisions that educational policy makers have to make today, regarding what really works best in choice of technology (Wagner et al. 2003).

Several important policy issues arise based on the information from the cost studies. The costs are significantly beyond households' ability to pay. Over 40% of rural households in Ghana fall under the government's defined poverty level, that is, "unacceptable physiological and social deprivation" (GPRS, 2003:6). The question is the sustainability of these ICT systems, even if government were to make the initial investment outlay.

The concern for sustainability has led to inquiry about rural households' willingness to pay for ICT services. For example, a survey under a Grameen Bank telephone project in rural Bangladesh revealed that "54% of member phone users indicated that they were willing to spend between 100 to 300 Taka ($2 to $6 USD) for a three minute phone call involving a financial matter with a family member overseas, and 27% said they were willing to spend between 300 to 600 Taka ($6 to $12.25 USD) for this kind of call. Given an average reported monthly income of 5,000 Taka ($102 USD) for respondents' households, these figures represent significant proportions of monthly household income, ranging from 2% to 12% (Quadir Iqbal, 2000, www.grameen.com DA: 10/20/04).

The concern over sustainability of ICT-use in rural areas raises a second policy issue concerning the choice of ICT infrastructure to adopt in a given location. Given that there are several ICT protocols (personal radio, community radio, telephone, television, etc), what factors could influence a household's choice of protocol? The literature suggests that cost is probably the driving factor. The idea of the "community radio," for example, seems targeted directly to reducing the cost of delivering information to rural households. The major international development agencies have spearheaded the community radio efforts. For example, the FAO Rural Radio and Simbani have developed content and training partnerships that use rural radio to raise awareness about issues critical to rural development.

Working with the World Association of Community Broadcasters (AMARC) and the Developing Countries Farm Radio Network (DCFRN), the FAO's rural radio programme focuses on helping to establish community radio stations, connecting these stations to the Internet, and training broadcasters to source information online. In addition, a dedicated web portal within FAO's World Agricultural Information Center (WAICENT) provides specialized content, including a warning service on food security for AMARC's news agency, "Simbani Africa." *Simbani*, which means 'talk' in ChiChewa, a language spoken in Malawi, Zambia and Mozambique, was launched in October 2003 and is a news service that focuses on human rights and democracy, gender and development, the environment, HIV/AIDS, and food security (http://www.fao.org /sd/ruralradio/en/index.html DA: 11/12/04).

Another community-based effort is the Rural Outreach Programme (ROP) in Uganda. The Uganda Media Women's Association, through its Rural Outreach Programme, uses a variety of information and communication strategies and tools to raise women's awareness about their rights. Women journalists visit ten rural districts four times a year to conduct participatory workshops on issues ranging from reproductive rights and constitutional rights to political and economic rights. Issues raised are often adapted into plays that are staged within the communities for a fee. Between visits, communities organize radio listening clubs to discuss programmes developed for rural populations. During field visits that last four or five days, women journalists record participants' experiences, and these are aired on Radio Uganda or published in local newspapers (http://www.simbani.amarc.org/ DA: 11/12/04).

Rapidly declining ICT prices have led to the use of fairly sophisticated approaches to address the issue of ICT use in rural settings. For instance, the use of the computer to create virtual classrooms at a distance is quite new and has not yet taken hold in most developing countries, including Ghana. Despite its newness, the practice has become quite common in industrialized countries. Relying extensively on the Internet and Web, virtual learning, where learners never meet their teacher or other students, can either supplement an existing face-to-face class or entirely replace the face-to-face experience (Dede 2004; Rudestam & Schoenholtz-Read, 2002; Zucker & Kozma, 2003, quoted by Wagner et al, 2003).

Some virtual experiences eliminate the teacher's role altogether or significantly reduce it. Virtual learning is beginning to be used in developing countries as well. One of the efforts is the African Virtual University (AVU) at the postsecondary level. Organized under World Bank auspices in 1997, AVU has established 31 learning centres in 17 developed countries, with one at the University of Ghana. Using a combination of online materials, online chat, video broadcasts, CD-ROMs and DVDs, the AVU has delivered over 3,000 hours of instructional programs to over 23,000 students (Wagner et al, 2003).

As explained by Wagner et al. (2003), an even more challenging advance is the possible use of speech recognition to address the cognitive needs of literacy learners, particularly those related to reading comprehension. The user speaks a word or phrase into a microphone hooked to a soundboard in the computer, and the computer matches the sound to a model sound pattern in its memory. After five minutes training, the software, which is available in several foreign languages, can create text documents from dictation at up to 160 words per minute. With the available second language tutorial software such as *Learn to Speak* (Broderbund: Novato, CA) series, learners read to a text word or respond to a question with a simple spoken response. The technology helps learners to build relatively simple speaking skills.

Text-to-speech is another technology with commercial applications like *Coolspeaking* (Peach Seed Software: Powder Springs, GA), which can read text from emails, web pages, or typed text. *Keystone Screen Speaker* (Words Worldwide Limited: Newcastle upon Tyne, UK) is a screen reader program that allows users to highlight text and have it read back to them, word by word, sentence by sentence, or paragraph by paragraph.

10
A MODEL FOR USING ICT FOR EMPOWERMENT OF RURAL WOMEN THROUGH ADULT EDUCATION

INTRODUCTION

One major gap in the literature on rural adult education for women is the lack of rigorous theoretical models or paradigms which would help explain the relationship between Information and Communication Technologies (ICT's), government policies, and individual household characteristics, as well as the empowerment to strengthen these relationships. This lack of a theoretical framework makes it difficult to extract testable hypotheses as inputs when planning and managing ICT resources in support of rural adult education among women. This is not to deny the contribution of authors who have empirically examined the effects of the socioeconomic characteristics on household decision-making and use of information. This chapter presents a theoretical framework which links ICT's, government policies, Adult Education, individual household characteristics, and empowerment among women.

THE MODEL

A framework explaining the relationship between information technologies, Adult Education and rural household information, and that advances women's empowerment, must at a minimum address five important issues. First, the framework must address the process of information technology policy formation and implementation. Second, the model must explore alternative information delivery technologies and recognize the cost and sustainability of those alternatives. Third, there is a need to recognize that rural women's choice of information technology is not only a technical issue, but, more importantly, it depends on the socio-economic characteristics of the women, especially their willingness and ability to pay for the technology. Fourth, the framework must point to selected indices that are general enough to capture the broad meaning of the concept of *empowerment among women*. And last, the framework must contain a feedback loop that highlights the critical role of information in the learning process. This last characteristic of the framework emphasizes the need to treat information availability and decision-making as an ongoing process and not a one-time event unrelated to the future choices of rural women.

The framework suggested in this study makes two important contributions to the existing literature on information technology and empowerment of Ghana's rural women and rural women in developing countries. First, this study extends an earlier framework suggested in a work by Vikas Nath (2001), in which was discussed the relationship between *information availability* and the empowerment of women. Nath's study does not explicitly show the modes of information delivery, the learning processes or the importance of socioeconomic factors and resources (human and material) in the empowerment process. This gap is filled in the following framework. The second contribution is built upon a suggestion by Professor Christopher Dede, of Harvard University, who remarked that the essence of the empowerment process is the ability of rural households to *learn* from the information made available to them. Thus there is a *feedback loop* that goes back to the policy planning level. Note the following graphic, which illustrates this feedback process:

ICTs for Empowerment of Rural Women through Adult Education

PROJECT PARTNERS

The basic policy decision regarding the use of ICT and Adult Education for empowerment of rural women is the outcome of a consultation process involving the central government, development partners, national research institutions, rural households, and civil society. The consultation process is especially critical because it is now firmly established that projects to address poverty are likely to fail unless those who would be affected by the projects become owners and participants in decisions at all phases of the planning and implementation.

The idea of *stakeholder participation* in policy planning is the cornerstone of Ghana's democratization process and explains why the Local Government Act (1988) and PNDC Law 207 decentralized the administrative machinery in Ghana to promote effective governance in fighting poverty. Consistent with the vision in Ghana's 1992 Constitution to promote participatory democracy, this Law divided the country into 110 administrative districts. Article 35 of the constitution states: "The state shall make democracy a reality by decentralizing the administration and financial machinery of government to regions and districts and by providing all possible opportunities to the people to participate in decision making at every level of national life and in government."

The approach used in the widely acclaimed *Ghana Poverty Reduction Strategy Paper* (GPRSP 2003) defined the *consultation process* to be very inclusive; thus, in this instance, *government* refers to the central, district and local authorities. Government also includes the chiefs and traditional authorities that (directly or indirectly) affect decision- making in rural areas. Ghana's poverty reduction process involved consultations with members of Parliament, with sector ministers and their deputies, and with District Assemblies (GPRSP 2003).

The development partners are major contributors to rural development programs in Ghana and other developing countries. According to the U.S. Agency for International Development (USAID), development partners are working in at least 14 sectors, including health, education, and governance. In 2001, grants and concessional loans to Ghana from over twenty multilateral and bilateral agencies amounted to about $919 million. According to USAID reports, U.S. assistance targeted education, health, family planning, and governance. The World Bank targeted infrastructure, education, and health. The International Monetary Fund focused on structural adjustment. Japan emerged as the largest bilateral donor with programs in education, health, and agriculture. The European Union supported transportation infrastructure. Great Britain, the second largest bilateral donor, assisted with programs in public administration, health, education, rural infrastructure and agriculture. Denmark focused on health, energy, and water (http://www.usaid.gov/pubs/cbj2003/afr/gh/ DA 02/08/2005). Similarly, in addition to internally generated funds, in its three-year Implementation Plan, the Ministry of Women and Children of Ghana

(MOWAC) sought to obtain 40% of its required funds from its development partners. Again, the Plan acknowledged the role of stakeholders, and, to enhance information-sharing and joint implementation, took strategic steps to collaborate with development partners (MOWAC 2005). It is against this background that any program targeting rural adult education and ICT's must take into consideration the immense contribution and participation of development partners.

Being major players in education policy planning and implementation, NGOs play an important role in giving *voice* to the poor in rural areas. A recent report, "Ghana NGO Alternative Report For Beijing + 10," (2004), by the *Network for Women's Rights in Ghana* (NETRIGHT), listed 26 NGO's whose activities affect the participation of women in the political process through policy legal reforms http://www.wildaf-ao.org/eng/IMG/doc/Ghana_ENG-2.doc (DA 02/08/2005). The report and the activities of the NGO's focused on seven critical issues directly related to the empowerment of women: 1) education and the girl-child, 2) health and environment, 3) power sharing and decision-making, 4) violence, 5) peace and human rights, 6) institutional mechanisms for the Advancement of Women, and 7) Women, Media and ICTs.

Civil Society is broadly defined to include the rural women; community members and groups; the media; trade unions; professional bodies; student unions; and the private sector. The GPRSP held consultations with 36 community organizations during the preparatory phase (GPRSP, 7). Given the burden on the government's budget, the private sector is critical in this framework, as it represents a major source for the development and adoption of new technologies. The roles of research institutions are especially critical in the proposed model. The term *Research institutions* refers to universities, polytechnics and other educational institutions. The ability to collect, process, and disseminate information is critical in decision-making in a society committed to using scientific information in public policy-making. The GPRSP process recognized the important role science-based information plays and devoted a one day seminar to the evaluation of comments from research institutions and policy think tanks (GPRSP 8).

In summary, the framework considers the emergence of a technology-based rural women's empowerment program to be the outcome of the interaction between government; donors; rural households; civil society; research institutions, and the private sector.

DISSEMINATION INSTRUMENTS – INFORMATION AND COMMUNICATION TECHNOLOGIES

The outcome of the deliberation between the policy-setting groups may be disseminated to rural women using a single technology or a combination of several technologies; in this framework these technologies are designated as *dissemination instruments*. These instruments are broadly defined to include both current and future technologies which, depending on the extent of policy commitment and support, could be used in the future. Holmes (2004) explains that ICT's are tools that facilitate the sharing of information and foster communication, and include both new and traditional information and communication technologies. She adds that while the emphasis is often on the new, on personal computers and the Internet; on the World Wide Web; on mobile phones, satellite and wireless technologies, an African ICT tool kit for development should embrace and encompass traditional forms of media, including telephone, radio, television, print media like newsletters, cartoons and graphic posters, and community communication initiatives such as listening groups and community theatre.

At the UN World Summit on the Information Society (WSIS), in Geneva in 2003, under the theme ICT4D (Information and Communication for Development) (<http://www.itu.int/wsis/> DA: 05/05/05), it was further observed that ICT's are part of the day-to-day reality of a rapidly increasing number of people everywhere. However, information and communication technologies provide new opportunities only for those who are literate, have a good education and adequate resources, while disadvantaged and marginalized groups have little chance to automatically benefit. This situation further increases social divides; it widens the gap between rich and poor countries and regions, between individuals, and even between men and women.

Meanwhile, there is a growing recognition that ICT is a powerful tool that can make development effective on a larger scale for disadvantaged people, because increasing numbers of development organizations globally use ICT to promote development and empowerment, increase participation, and reduce poverty (Fust 2004). Similarly, Mali's former Minister of Education and President of the World Summit on Information Society (WSIS) Preparatory Committee, Adama Samassekou, concluded at the Summit that the "ICT for Development Platform has made it clear to everybody that we need to start sharing knowledge and information at once if we want to bridge the many divides which separate rich from poor, urban from rural, men from women, majorities from minorities and young from old" (Waldburger and Weigel 2004, 9). At the international level, it has been observed that women could benefit greatly if they were empowered with information communication technology. In line with the observations of the World Bank Group, WSIS and Holmes among others, the framework considers ICT infrastructure or dissemination instruments to include the print media, telephones, radios and televisions.

In terms of the print media, the focus is on extension bulletins and adult education publications, which are assumed to be part of a person-to-person information delivery protocol. Given the current low level circulation (about 14 per 1000 population in 2001, compared to about 40 per thousand population for low-income countries for the same period), the framework does not directly include newspapers (World Bank, *Development Data Group 2003).*

The use of radio in rural communication is very common and popular in Sub-Sahara Africa (SSA), thus the proposed framework considers radio technology to be a key information delivery instrument. Ghana has one of the highest radio ownership rates in SSA, 710 per 1,000 people in 2002, compared to an ownership rate of 198 per 1,000 people in the rest of SSA, and 139 per 1,000 people for all low income countries. Ghana's ownership rate represents an approximate increase of 207% over the 7-year period of 1995-2002 (World Bank, *Development Data Group 2003*). Following an approach used in several studies, information dissemination via radio is considered in two contexts, i.e., private radio and community radio. Private radio is owned by individuals; community radio is placed popular sites, such as town halls or community centers, where people can gather to listen to programs.

There are good reasons to consider radio use in these two contexts. Governments and development partners (who usually fund the rural education programs) may want to reduce the cost of information dissemination by increasing the number of radio listeners per radio. An added benefit of the community radio approach is that it affords an opportunity for listeners to *interact and react* to broadcast information and thus takes into account the views and opinions of the group. This interaction enriches the learning process and may be preferred by many households.

On the other hand, there might be some rural households that prefer to receive information on their own private radio. It is plausible that younger people and educated adults may want to have the freedom to listen to other radio programs (for example, broadcasts in English), and therefore will be more willing to pay for their own radio rather than paying for a community radio. It is also very likely that educated rural dwellers have higher incomes, since they may generate income from both farm and non-farm sources, and thus may be in a position to pay for their own radio sets and receive information privately.

IMPLEMENTATION AGENCY - ADULT EDUCATION

Adult education, irrespective of the content, focuses on any educational program organized for adults. The increasing use of radio, network television, and cable television for educating adults is a major development. Broadcast media are now being used worldwide to provide public information, to teach reading and writing, to make available specialized seminars and short courses, and to provide university-degree programs. The electronic media offer the means for reaching populations that are homebound or geographically isolated, rural communities.

In Ghana, the Non-Formal Education Division (NFED) of the Ministry of Education is the machinery by which the Government delivers basic adult functional literacy. Launched in 1991, the National Functional Literacy Program has undertaken several activities to accelerate the reduction of illiteracy, and to facilitate rural and national development. A report by the NFED on the celebration of the International Literacy Day (2005), indicates that the National Functional Literacy Program provides reading, writing, and numeracy, in an enabling environment where learners acquire income-generating skills necessary for such income-generation activities as cassava processing, bakery, batik and tie-dying, weaving, and bee-keeping. There is also an English literacy program to supplement the teaching of local language skills. Some students have graduated into the formal educational system and proceeded through to the tertiary level. Others have also taken responsible roles in the communities to serve as Traditional Birth Attendants, religious leaders, District Assembly persons and Unit Committee chairpersons (NFED 2005).

A literate population is a necessity for any nation wishing to take advantage of modern technological growth. Research has shown a direct relationship between literacy among women and improved family health and child care. The United Nations Educational, Scientific and Cultural Organization (UNESCO) has long supported the concept that education must be considered an ongoing process and therefore encourages literacy programs, agricultural extension, and community instruction. In light of this, using information and communication technologies adult education becomes crucial for facilitating empowerment among rural women.

TARGET AUDIENCE - RURAL WOMEN

The target audience in this framework is rural women who utilize information for decision-making towards empowerment. These women reside in rural communities with limited infrastructural developments, i.e., poor road networks, poor health facilities, lack of hydro-electric power, and are mainly engaged in the informal job sector in areas such as agriculture; in aggregate these circumstances lead to a low socio-economic status (by both national and international standards). By these standards, the women are often characterized as poor: they operate mainly in the informal sector; they are predominantly agricultural with low educational status; they have poor health; they have limited access to infrastructural developments; and they face numerous developmental challenges. It is estimated that 56% of the Ghanaian population live in rural areas, with women constituting about 51% of the rural population (GPRSP, 13). The socio-economic, political and cultural conditions within which this population makes decisions is a crucial determinate in their willingness to pay for and use information with which to improve decision-making opportunities.

With women constituting about 51% of the rural population, a coherent ICT policy for rural information delivery could affect a sizable population, since about 56% of the Ghanaian population has been defined to live in a rural area. Nearly 48.7% self-employed women engaged in agriculture are classified as poor, while about 45.1% of the self-employed in non-agricultural activities are defined as poor. Some of the critical socio-economic characteristics of rural households, and their potential implication for a household's technology choice in the Ghanaian setting, are discussed below.

SOCIO-ECONOMIC CHARACTERISTICS AND TECHNOLOGY CHOICE

1. *Income:* It is difficult to predict the effect of income on the willingness to use and pay for ICT in rural households; generally, a positive relationship between income and the willingness to use and pay for ICT is expected. Households with high incomes tend to spend a smaller proportion of income on food, while poorer households spend a higher proportion of income on food. One would expect the effect of income on ICT to be positive in the rural communities of relatively richer regions, since they may have some extra money after meeting their basic needs of food, clothing, and shelter, and other essential needs and activities. Furthermore, one would expect households with high incomes to use private radios instead of community radios in receiving information.

It could be argued that even though poorer households spend a higher proportion of income on basic needs like food, their interest in obtaining information to *jumpstart* their way out of poverty may increase their willingness to pay for ICT information. In essence, there might not be statistically significant differences in households' willingness to use and pay across regions, so it is difficult to predict with a high degree of certainty the exact sign (positive or negative) on the income variable, thus the issue is left to empirical determination.

2. *Education:* Table 5. 1 reinforces the need to focus on rural female education in the fight against poverty. Rural females have lower school attendance rates across all regions, with the lowest rates recorded in the three northern regions of Ghana (Northern, Upper West and Upper East). Generally, given the premium on information in decision- making, it is hypothesized that educated households will be willing to pay for and use any ICT media. While an illiterate household naturally would depend on the radio and extension visits for information, a literate household has additional sources of information delivered through extension bulletins and other printed sources.

3. *Age:* It is hypothesized that older heads-of-households will be more likely to use and pay for community radio systems and extension visits, and there are good reasons for this assumption. First, older heads-of-households are likely to belong to community organizations, and hence would be more comfortable with sharing the media. On the other hand, a young household is likely to be less involved in community organizations and would be willing to choose their own private radio system.

Table 5. 1 Proportion of adults in region based on school, by sex and locality (%)

Region	Urban			Rural			Ghana		
	Male	Female	All	Male	Female	All	Male	Female	All
Western	91.5	79.4	84.8	87.3	58.2	72.0	88.3	63.6	75.2
Central	84.1	64.6	72.6	79.2	54.5	64.9	80.6	57.5	67.1
Greater Accra	93.0	80.4	86.6	85.8	61.9	72.5	92.6	79.1	85.6
Volta	89.8	70.4	80.1	80.4	55.0	67.0	82.7	58.5	70.2
Eastern	87.7	74.6	80.2	86.3	62.3	73.5	86.6	65.1	74.9
Ashanti	92.6	82.6	86.7	88.8	64.8	75.5	90.2	72.1	80.0
Brong Ahafo	85.8	69.1	75.9	83.9	58.4	70.8	84.4	61.9	72.3
Northern	59.4	20.1	41.4	42.6	23.0	32.8	46.0	22.5	34.5
Upper West	56.2	56.2	56.2	52.3	23.8	38.7	53.6	34.8	44.5
Upper East	85.7	50.0	66.7	29.6	12.3	21.0	35.7	16.9	26.3
All	87.8	73.8	80.2	74.5	51.5	62.4	79.2	59.6	68.8

Source: GLSS 4 (Table 2.3).

4. *Marriage:* Married women are likely to be more willing to pay for and use private radio media. The basis for this assertion is that married women are more confined to private life. Several socio-cultural factors affect their level of participation in public life and interaction with strangers. In addition, child care, home care and other domestic activities form the priority of married rural women's engagements, all of which limit their ability to engage in leisure and other empowering socio-economic and public activities. Limited by these inhibiting factors, they are likely to prefer to have their own private radios. Another factor contributing to married women's willingness to use and pay for private radios could be that married women may have higher income (spouses combined income) and could therefore afford the more expensive media for information delivery.

5. *Household Size*: The household in this study is defined to include all persons who are under the direct responsibility of a female head. At a given income level, large households are less likely to use and pay for private radios given the cost of these radios. While large households will be more willing to use and pay for community radios and extension services, small households are more likely to be willing to use and pay for private radios due to the increasing expenditure levels associated with increasing family size.

6. *Membership of Community Organizations*: It is hypothesized that households who belong to a community organization will be willing to choose information delivered via community radio. Community radio is cheaper than a

private radio, and more importantly, these households have cultivated the spirit of sharing through their membership in an organization. Table 4.2 shows that rural households make more contribution to community initiatives than do urban households. By analogy, it is hypothesized that households in the more deprived areas (especially in the northern regions) will be more willing to use and pay for community radio and extension services, compared to those rural communities located near the urbanized regions of Ghana, such as Accra, Kumasi (Ashanti), Takoradi (Western), Cape Coast (central).

A summary of the questions for investigation will therefore include the following;

1. Are female household heads with high income willing to pay for information media?
2. Will educated women be more willing to pay for information media?
3. Will older women be more willing to pay for community radio systems?
4. Are married women likely to be more willing to pay for private radio media?
5. Are large households more willing to pay for community radios?
6. Will women belonging to community organizations be willing to pay for community radio systems?

Table 5. 2. Miscellaneous Expenditures by Urban and Rural Households

	Mean household expenditure			Estimated total miscellaneous expenditure
	Urban	Rural	All	
Purpose of expenditure	(cedis)			(billion cedis)
Taxes (TV License, property tax etc.)	3,700	1,300	2,200	8.8
Contributions to self-help projects	9,500	10,200	9,900	40.4
Weddings, dowry, funeral, etc.	91,900	62,900	73,500	298.9
Gifts and presents (excluding remittances)	36,700	28,900	31,800	129.3
Other miscellaneous expenditures	21,500	12,500	15,800	64.3
Total	163,300	115,800	133,200	541.7

Source: GLSS 4 (Table 9. 27)

EMPOWERMENT GOALS AND THE FEEDBACK LOOP

Information obtained through Adult Education (from any of the media sources) is to be used to empower rural women with increased educational and job opportunities; income growth; improved health; gender equity; and political participation. And, more broadly, education enables rural women to contribute to global competition, a goal which is in line with the Millennium Development Goals (MDG's). Seven of the MDG's are directly associated with how careful policies and programs help to improve the overall well-being of women in society: 1) eradication of extreme poverty and hunger; 2) universal primary education; 3) gender equality and women's empowerment; (4 reduction in child mortality; 5) improvements in maternal health care; 6) combating HIV/AIDS, malaria, and other diseases; and 7) environmental sustainability. In Ghana, a review of the MDG's +5 showed that though much progress has been made in these core areas of women's empowerment, so much more needs to be done to advance the total empowerment of the rural woman. Within the context of International Commitments (particularly the African and Beijing Platforms for Action, Beijing+5 and 10, the MDGs and MOWAC) Ghana has decided to focus on ten core areas:

1. Women and Poverty
2. Education and Training of Women
3. Women and the Economy
4. Women in Power and Decision-making
5. Institutional mechanisms for the Advancement of Women
6. Human Rights of Women
7. Women and the Media
8. Women and the Environment
9. The Girl-Child

In its Strategic Implementation Plan (2005 – 2008), MOWAC plans to consolidate the efforts being made in these core areas of women's empowerment (MOWAC 2005). All strategies have achievement indicators and costs attached which serve as signals to the decision-making bodies to revise policies and plans to improve the living conditions of rural women. Thus the feedback loop in the framework is intended to emphasize the ongoing and long-term nature of the empowerment process. As previously cited, the result of this process is to achieve their empowerment goals (participation in the political process, income and growth, jobs). The essence of the empowerment process is the ability of rural households to learn from the information made available to them, and the result of the learning process is reflected in the decisions made by households. More significantly, the lesson from the learning process then becomes an input in subsequent policy planning, and generates new information which informs the future decisions of rural women. In essence, the framework explicitly recognizes learning as an important component of the women's empowerment process.

CONCLUSION

A key to successful policy planning and implementation is to give rural women (whose lives will be affected by decisions concerning ICT) a voice at the planning stage. A *top down* approach that neglects the views and wishes of rural dwellers is likely to lead to a waste of resources since the critical factor of *ownership* would be absent. Rural women are likely to adopt and use information when such information and the media reflect their interests and aspirations. In regard to Adult Education strategies and programs, it is imperative that the assumptions, expectations and hypotheses explaining the relationship between rural women's willingness to pay for and use selected information delivery technologies, which would lead to their empowerment, could no doubt be subjected to empirical verification using survey data to obtain empirical analyses by asking and answering the these questions:

1. Are female household's heads with high income willing to pay for information media?
2. Will educated women be more willing to pay for information media?
3. Will older women be more willing to pay for community radio systems?
4. Are married women likely to be more willing to pay for private radio media?
5. Are large households more willing to pay for community radios?
6. Will women belonging to community organizations be willing to pay for community radio systems?
7. Will women belonging to community organizations be willing to pay for community radio systems?

The following chapter gives a report of the study that responds to these questions.

11
ICT'S AND ADULT EDUCATION FOR RURAL WOMEN: ASSESSING WILLINGNESS TO PAY FOR INFORMATION DELIVERY

INTRODUCTION

Recognizing the need to use information and communication technologies to make information accessible to rural women, and the financial implications and possible challenges to rural women, it became necessary to assess Ghana's rural women's willingness to pay for ICT protocols. The research process, the instrument for data collection and research report are presented in this chapter.

THE SURVEY

In order to develop the survey instrument used to collect the primary data used in estimating the quantitative impact of the variables hypothesized to influence households' willingness to pay for information, the information from the literature survey was combined with key elements of the general framework.

The data used in this study was based on a contingent valuation survey instrument administered in several villages in Ghana. The survey instrument was divided into two main parts (see Appendix 1).

Part One sought information on basic characteristics of households, specifically, marital status, dependents, occupation, education, expenditures, and membership in community organizations. For analytical purposes, age of respondents was re-organized into two major age groupings, those aged 0-20, and those aged 21 and above. Similarly, the educational levels were re-grouped into primary and above primary.

Part Two consisted of a bidding game for alternative information delivery technologies. Three main information delivery technologies were considered; community radio, private radio, and extension agent. The main distinguishing features of these technologies were price and mode of delivery. For example, since several households contributed to the purchase and maintenance of the community radio system, (information delivery by community radio where a group of women could meet at a learning center to listen to and discuss a program), this option was considered the least expensive. Extension agents were considered the second least costly of the three technologies, and was considered so because the government pays these agents to move from one community and household to another to provide technical information and support. The objective was to explore the extent to which a part of the cost of extension information delivery could be shifted to households and lessen the burden on government. Since a household owns the private technology system and thus assumes the full amount of the cost, the third and most expensive delivery technology system was the private radio.

Bidding took the form of a series of specific questions. For example, a respondent was asked whether she would be willing to pay ¢1,000 per year to use a community radio. If the answer was in the affirmative, the question was posed again with incremental increases to ¢2,000. The process continued until there was a *No* answer. The final amount to which the respondent answered *yes* was recorded as the *maximum willingness to pay amount* for community village radio installation. For extension agents, the beginning bid was at ¢5,000; for private radios, the beginning point was ¢10,000. Respondents were also asked to state an amount they were willing to pay for each of the information delivery technologies.

Field data was collected with the assistance of the Regional Program Organizers of the Institute of Adult Education, at all ten of Ghana's Regional Centers, all of which are constantly engaged with the local people in community programs. These field officers were recruited for this survey because they are in partnership with the community members, and who have (over time) won the confidence and trust of the rural households; developed a good knowledge of the regional demographics; established mutual working relationships with the women in the local communities, and become able to communicate in the language that the people understand. Their accumulated community research, training experience, residence in the regions, and effort helped to quickly and accurately collect field data. Data were collected in face-to-face interviews in which the interviewer had the opportunity to explain to the respondent the purpose of the survey, and the need to obtain truthful responses.

The interviewers were quite familiar with the villages, and, based on their experiences, understood the need to interview in a manner that did not impair the integrity of the effort. They interviewed the female household head of every-other house. Where the female household heads were absent in a designated house, they moved to the next house (in the every-other house sequence) until they had interviewed and obtained data from the requisite 100 respondents. Respondents were cautioned not to discuss their responses with other households. There was broad agreement among field staff that the respondents took the process seriously and willingly offered truthful information to assist in achieving the objectives of the survey.

To analyze the data on the socio-economic characteristics of the respondents in frequencies and percentages, Statistical Package for Social Sciences (SPSS 12.0) was used and the results presented in tables and graphs. On households' willingness to pay for alternative information delivery technologies, a contingent valuation (CV) method was used to quantitatively estimate the influence of selected socio-economic factors. CV methods have been applied to several public goods valuations in developing countries. For example, Thobani (1983), Tan et al., and Mingat (1984) used the approach to study payments for education services, Jimenez to study health service payments; Boadu to study rural water supply; Haba (2004) to study rural information services, and Whittington to study rural water supplies. Even though the method does not answer several important questions (including ability to pay and equity concerns), it has been widely accepted as a useful tool to help planners gain some understanding in establishing basic financing guidelines in the provision of public goods. The analysis was intended to provide basic information regarding rural households' willingness to pay for information delivery technologies. For information delivery, the data from the survey were used in a linear regression model to obtain quantitative estimates of the impact of the identified socio-economic factors on households' willingness to pay for three technologies, i.e., community radio, private radio, and extension agents. The multiple linear regression relationship was assumed between the dependent variable and the independent variables.

Results of the analysis are presented below. The first part presents results on the socio-economic description of the respondents, while the second part provides regression results of the quantitative estimation of the data from the ten regions.

Summary of Dependent and Independent Variables

Dependent Variable   **Independent variables**

- Yearly expenses on basic necessities (food, shelter, education, medication etc)

Willingness to pay   - Level of education
(amount of money)   - Age
- Marital status
- Number of dependants
- Membership in a Community organization

PART I: DESCRIPTION OF SOCIO-ECONOMIC
CHARACTERISTICS OF RESPONDENTS

Age

Table 6.1 shows the age distribution of respondents. From the results, it could be observed that a higher percentage (about 94%) of the respondents fell within the active adult stage of 21 to 50 years, persons assumed to be in their peak stage of development and production. Their responses could well inform policy on the use of ICT for rural adult education and the willingness to pay for such facility and services.

Table 6 1. Age Distribution of Respondents

Age	Frequency	Percent
Up to 20	54	5.4
21 – 30	308	30.8
31 – 40	286	28.6
41 – 50	198	19.8
Above 50	147	14.7
No response	7	.7
Total	1000	100

Source: Survey Data, 2004/5

Marital Status

From Figure 6.1 below it could be observed that typical of a Ghanaian rural community, a majority (almost 70%) of the household heads were married. Considering rural women's socio-cultural roles and their status as women/wives, and the nature of the cultural male - female relationship, husbands could be significant players in adult women's education programs, and thus their views, consent, and support will be crucial for effective program planning and implementation. The 29.3% of unmarried, heads-of-households indicates that these single parents will likely have more financial responsibilities and therefore are less willing to pay for an adult education program.

Figure 6. 1. Marital Status of Respondents

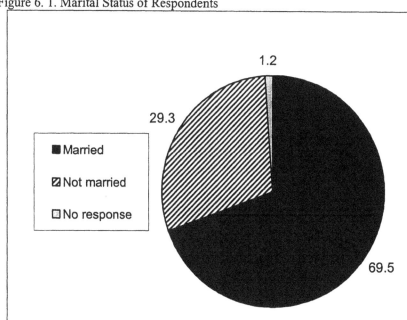

Source: Survey Data, 2004/5

Dependants of Respondents

To indicate the extent of their financial commitments, respondents were asked to indicate their number of dependents. By definition, dependents meant not only their biological daughters and sons, but all their wards or other people for whom they were responsible, and Table 6.2 provides the detailed results. Typical of a rural Ghanaian household, the number of dependents ranged from 0 to 17. Nevertheless, it is impressive to note that the majority of the respondents (88.3%) had a total number of dependents ranging from 0 to 6. Breaking it down further, it was observed that over 55% had a total number of dependents ranging from 0 to 3 (Table 6.2). If the number of one's dependents impacts on the level of one's financial commitments, this result shows that the majority of the household heads (55%) who had fewer dependents could somehow be able to invest in their personal development if they wished to do so.

Sources of Income of Respondents

Amazingly, the majority of the household heads had regular sources of income which included farming, trading, dressmaking, hairdressing, teaching, and office work. As shown in Table 6, unemployment is very low (11.2%) among the household heads. In addition, the results showed that 62.4% of the respondents indicated that apart from their regular jobs, they had other sources of income. This result strengthens the point that the household heads could have some ability to contribute to an information technology for rural adult education.

Level of Education

Formal educational attainment appears to be very low among the female rural household heads. Figure 6.2 below shows that a sizeable figure (45%) of the household heads had no formal education. Only 1.1% had attained tertiary education. Therefore, it is not surprising to note that only 5.3% of the rural women were engaged in formal jobs like teaching and office work (Table 6.3). This makes a *specially designed* adult education program for the rural women very crucial. For effective personal development and decision-making, these rural women will need information presented in their vernacular and in a medium with which they will be comfortable.

Table 6. 2. Number of Dependents of Respondents

Source	Frequency	Percentage
0 – 3	558	55.8
4 – 6	325	32.5
7 – 9	81	8.1
10 – 12	22	2.2
13 – 17	7	.7
No response	7	.7
Total	1000	100

Source: Survey Data, 2004/5

Table 6. 3. Sources of Income of Respondents

Source	Frequency	Percentage
Farming	239	23.9
Trading	458	45.8
Dressmaking	77	7.7
Hairdressing	41	4.1
Teaching	27	2.7
Office worker	26	2.6
Other	20	2.0
None	112	11.2
Total	1000	100

Source: Survey Data, 2004/5

Figure 6.2: Levels of Education of Respondents

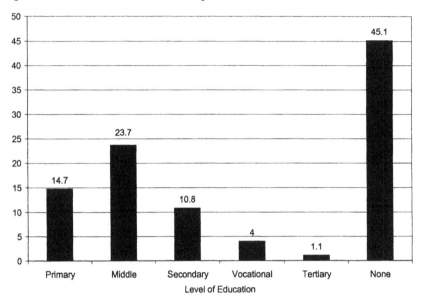

Source: Survey Data, 2004/5

INFORMATION ACQUISITION

As knowledge of the information acquisition status of the rural female house-hold heads could be useful for assessing their willingness to pay for a facility or service for informing and empowering them, a section of the survey instrument was structured to elicit this data. A remarkable aspect of rural women is their sense of communalism, of belonging and sharing, and they seem to draw more energy and motivation from participation in group activities. Membership of the household heads in women's groups or societies was therefore explored from the survey. The results revealed that 50.3% of the rural women were members of women's groups and cooperatives, indicating that some of the women may be willing to access a shared, group-learning media. To the question as to whether the women received information on agriculture, trading, health, education, and government, 49.7% responded in the affirmative, showing that nearly half of the household heads do receive such information. However, one cannot determine the intensity, usefulness, and applicability of such information. A higher per-centage (72.5%) indicated their desire to acquire information and skills, which is a good indicator of the need for a *specially designed,* rural adult program for the women.

As to whether participants pay to receive information, 7.6% responded that they pay for information delivery. On the average, the amounts they quoted ranged from ¢5.000 to ¢10.000. This could probably be for telecommunication services. Meanwhile, the willingness to pay for a special adult education program for women was very high. From the results, 77.6% indicated that they would be willing to pay for the learning media if the government offered such a specially-designed program, while 4.8% were not sure of their decision. Similarly, 79.3% indicated their willingness to pay for such a facility if it is offered by a private organization.

In finding out who should be responsible for paying the cost of information technology, respondents indicated that it should be the Government (21%), or District Assemblies (6%), or Non-governmental organizations (4%), but the majority (69%) of the respondents indicated that it was the responsibility of the individuals using the facility to pay for it.

It could be extrapolated and summarised from the above that:

- A majority of the household heads (94%) were in their active adult stage of 21 to 50 years.
- Almost 70% of the household heads were married, making the consent and support of spouses crucial for effective program design and implementation.
- Over 55% had the total number of their dependents ranging from 0 – 3.
- Unemployment appeared to be low among the rural women.
- Almost 89% had regular sources of income.
- Regarding educational attainment, 45% of the household heads had no formal education, making a specially-designed adult education program very necessary.
- 50.3% of the rural women were members of women's groups and co-operatives, indicating the possibility of a group-based activity.
- A higher percentage of 72.5 indicated their desire to acquire information and skills.
- Over 75% indicated their willingness to pay for the learning media if the government or private organizations were to offer such a program.

PART II: STATISTICAL ESTIMATION AND RESULTS

A multiple linear regression relationship was assumed between the dependent variable and the independent variables. The mathematical expression of the relationship for households in each region is as follows:

1. $(WTP)_{ijt} = a_0 + a_1 (AGE) + a_2 (EDUC) + a_3 (MARS) + a_4 (DEPEND) + a_5 (EXPEND) + a6 (MEMBR) + U_i,$

$(WTP)_{ijt}$ is the willingness to pay by a household (i) in region (j) for information delivery technology (t), AGE is age of respondent measured in years, EDUC is the educational level of respondent. To reflect the varied forms of education encountered in rural households, the educational level was broken down into primary, secondary, vocational, and technical parts, but was regrouped into up to primary and above primary for analytical purposes. MARS is the marital status of respondent, and was measured using a *dummy* variable equal to 1 if respondent is married, and zero if not. DEPEND is the number of dependents of respondent; EXPEND is the aggregate of all expenditures reported by the respondent measured in Ghana Cedis, and MEMBR is the membership of respondent in a community organization. Membership was measured as a *dummy* variable, equal to 1 if the respondent belonged to a community organization, and zero otherwise. The term U is a random error term assumed N (0, σ^2).

ESTIMATION TECHNIQUE

Equation 1 was estimated for each individual region using the Newey-West estimator, an estimation technique that helps to address one of the common problems inherent in cross-section data usage. The socio-economic characteristics of households differ in important ways, so unless the statistical procedure takes into account these variations, the estimated coefficients may not be efficient due to problems of *heteroskedasticity* and *autocorrelation*. To give consistent and efficient estimates, the Newey-West estimation procedure takes into account the problems in using cross-section data. The results of the estimation procedures are presented in Table 6.4 which lists the means of selected independent variables for the ten regions in the study, and the mean bids for extension services, community and private radio. Mean household size and expenditures are also provided. Consistent with expectation, mean bids for private radio is highest, followed by mean bids for extension information, followed by community radio.

Table 6.4 Means of Independent Variables Compared to Means from GLSS 4

Region	Commu- nity Radio	Pri- vate Radio	Exten- sion Agent	No. of Depend- ents	Expendi- ture Survey	Expendi- ture GLSS 4
Western	3535.5	10404	6182	2.79	5,052,525	4,677,000
Ashanti	3360	22300	8480	3.61	11,054,650	5,008,000
B. Ahafo	3730	24305	10030	1.77	4,180,710	3,544,000
Central	3886	22450	10180	3.74	5,153,510	2,977,000
Eastern	4868	22696	8909	3.33	8,549,222	3,736,000
Gt. Accra	3656	21162	10202	2.83	11,495,487	6,777,000
Northern	3400	21069	9520	4.43	3,335,400	2,837,000
Upper East	3141	21262	8595	3.04	4,059,460	1,793,000
Upper East	3830	26200	9980	5.67	2,070,160	2,462,000
Volta	5200	11190	7320	2.39	6,134,540	4,000,000

Source: Survey and GLSS 4, Table 9.2

Mean expenditure pattern for households also tracks the numbers from GLSS 4. However, in the Greater Accra, Eastern, and Central regions, means from the survey significantly differ from the means based on GLSS 4. Since the GLSS 4 is based on 1999 information, it could be that expenditures have changed significantly over the last five years. Nevertheless, the means are sufficiently credible to provide a reasonable basis for the survey data analysis.

Tables 6.5a, 6.5b, and 6.5c present the results of regression analysis using the combined data set for all regions. Four observations were rejected, thus the total number of observations is 996 instead of 1000 (100 observations for each of the 10 regions). The overall explanatory power of the model is poor with an R^2 (Coefficient of determination) of 7.5% for the community radio regression, 6.9% for private radio and 8.4% for extension services. The low explanatory power of the models is not fatal, especially given the consistency and statistical significance of several of the critical socio-economic factors that were hypothesized to influence rural women's willingness to pay for selected information delivery technologies.

Table 6.5a reveals that older women who are educated above the primary school level with high expenditure levels, and are members of a community organization, are more willing to pay for information delivered via a community radio. With the exception of the income factor, that is statistically significant at the 10% level; all the other factors are significant at the 1% and 5% levels. The Table also shows that younger women (below age 20) are not willing to pay for information delivered via a community radio. Results for information delivered via private radio (Table 6.5b) follow the pattern obtained for community radio, but it was also found that married women are willing to pay for information delivered via private radio. This may be due to the fact that married households have higher income (combined income) and could afford the more expensive media for information delivery.

This observation is supported by the fact that the estimated coefficient for expenditures (.00011) in Table 6.5b is larger than the estimated coefficient for expenditures (5.09E-06) in Table 6.5a. The expenditure factor in Table 6.5b is highly significant (1% level) compared to the significance level (5%) for the same factor in Table 6.5a. Table 6.5c reports the results of estimation for information delivered via extension agents. The pattern observed under the two previous results is observed for information delivery via extension agents. Here again the principal factors are high education, high expenditures, membership in community organizations, age and marital status. Once again the results show that younger women are not willing to pay for information delivered via extension agents. The only non significant in explaining variation in the choice of information media is the number of dependents.

Table 6.5a Regression Results for Households Willingness to Pay for Community Radio: All Regions

Variable	Coefficient	t-Statistic
Constant	3017.98	23.08
Age [Up to 20]	-704.62	-5.07
Age [Above 20]	180.84	2.69
Married	38.70	0.43
Dependents	-1.60	-0.10
Educ. [Primary]	-110.71	-0.84
Educ. [Above Primary]	187.74	2.05
Expenditure	5.09E-06	1.62
Membership	316.90	3.54
R-squared	0.075	N = 996

Table 6.5b Regression Results for Households Willingness to Pay for Private Radio: All Regions

Variable	Coefficient	t-Statistic
Constant	12333.05	8.14
Age [Up to 20]	-5469.63	-2.54
Age [Above 20]	1041.34	0.81
Married	3433.88	2.47
Dependents	348.89	1.40
Educ. [Primary]	1204.46	0.73
Educ. [Above Primary]	5663.57	3.17
Expenditure	0.00011	2.82
Membership	4867.08	3.69
R-squared	0.069	N = 996

Table 6.5c Regression Results for Households Willingness to Pay for Extension Officer: All Regions

Variable	Coefficient	t-Statistic
Constant	6707.23	17.23
Age [Up to 20]	-1855.98	-4.57
Age [Above 20]	395.12	1.95
Married	463.64	1.71
Dependents	48.58	1.059
Educ. [Primary]	-27.67	-0.089
Educ. [Above Primary]	473.32	1.82
Expenditure	1.43E-05	2.22
Membership	1298.57	5.20
R-squared	0.084	N = 996

ASHANTI REGION

Other than the expected low coefficient of determination when using cross-section data, the regression results for Ashanti region (Tables 6.6a, 6.6b, and 6.6c below) did not follow the pattern observed under the regressions using data for all regions. Only the expenditure variable was found to be significant in the regression for all information delivery media. Even though the estimated coefficients for the expenditure were small (2.34E-06 for community radio; 3.49E-05 for private radio; 9.31E-06 for extension services), they were all highly significant at the 1% level. In explaining the variation in households' willingness to pay, two other variables were found to be mildly important. Table 11a shows a positive relationship between the number of dependents and households' willingness to pay for information delivered via community radio. The estimated coefficient was significant at the 10% level. These results are consistent with the hypothesis of this study, that households with a large number of dependents spend more on household maintenance and would opt for the cheaper medium (community radio) for information delivery. The results for community radio also reveal that households with education above the primary level are not willing to pay for information delivered via community radio. The estimated coefficient of −1.89 is significant at the 10% level. It is not immediately clear why this outcome was obtained. One would have expected that since there is a positive relationship between expenditure and willingness to pay for information delivered via any media, educated households would value information and hence be more willing to pay.

Table 6.6a: Regression Results for Households' Willingness to Pay for Community Radio: Ashanti Region

Variable	Coefficient	t-Statistic
Constant	3369.005	11.43
Age [Up to 20]	-666.53	-1.51
Age [Above 20]	158.97	0.67
Married	-117.85	-0.37
Dependants	70.29	1.72
Educ. [Primary]	-526.86	-1.02
Educ. [Above Primary]	-378.76	-1.89
Expenditure	2.34E-06	2.51
Membership	105.99	0.27
R-squared	0.12	N = 100

Table 6.6b: Regression Results for Households' Willingness to Pay for Private Radio: Ashanti Region

Variable	Coefficient	t-Statistic
Constant	21702.51	6.11
Age [Up to 20]	5181.99	1.39
Age [Above 20]	-2787.089	-1.43
Married	-1200.54	-0.45
Dependents	-506.98	-1.14
Educ. [Primary]	-1873.002	-0.28
Educ. [Above Primary]	2771.096	1.25
Expenditure	3.49E-05	4.21
Membership	5696.46	1.83
R-squared	0.14	N = 100

Table 6.6c: Regression Results for Households' Willingness to Pay for Extension Agent: Ashanti Region

Variable	Coefficient	t-Statistic
Constant	9077.58	6.50
Age [Up to 20]	1863.68	1.43
Age [Above 20]	-1083.80	-1.57
Married	-536.63	-0.54
Dependents	-52.75	-0.38
Educ. [Primary]	472.70	0.18
Educ. [Above Primary]	424.38	0.31
Expenditure	9.31E-06	3.74
Membership	690.14	0.72
R-squared	0.084	N = 100

BRONG AHAFO REGION

Tables 6.7a, 6.7b, 6.7c summarize the effects of selected socio-economic factors on households' willingness to pay for information delivered via community radio, private radio, and by extension agents. The overall explanatory power of the models as measured by the R^2 (Coefficient of determination) is high, ranging from a high of 44% for extension agents to a low of 14% for community radio. The R^2 for private radio is 27%. There were no statistically significant factors explaining households' willingness to pay for community radio, even though the signs on some of the critical variables hypothesized to influence households' decisions were consistent with the hypothesis in the study. For example, there is a positive relationship between household expenditures and willingness to pay, and a negative relationship between the number of dependants and the willingness to pay. The results for community radio also show that while those with above-primary level education are willing to pay for community radio, those with lower education are not willing to pay for community radio. This may be due to the value placed on information by those with high education.

Table 6.7b shows that households at all educational levels are willing to pay for information delivered via private radio. The table also shows that households with high expenditures are willing to pay for information via private radio. These results are consistent with the hypotheses and support the proposition that the choice of media is important in the delivery of information to rural households. Since households with high expenditures are wealthier households, it is not surprising that a positive relationship is found between expenditures and willingness to pay for private radio. The results for private radio help to explain why households are not willing to pay for information delivered via community radio.

Table 6.7c shows the results for households' willingness to pay for information delivered via extension agents. Households with many dependents are not willing to pay for information delivered via extension services, and the estimated coefficient is significant at the 5% level. The negative relationship between the number of dependents and willingness to pay is found for all three methods of information delivery. There is a strong and statistically significant (1% level) relationship between household expenditures and willingness to pay for information delivered via extension services. For the Brong Ahafo region, what emerges is that efforts to empower rural women would entail a combination of approaches involving the availability of both private radios and extension services.

Table 6.7a Regression Results for Households Willingness to Pay for Community Radio: Brong Ahafo Region

Variable	Coefficient	t-Statistic
Constant	3931.46	3.12
Age [Up to 20]	6464.87	1.55
Age [Above 20]	361.55	0.28
Married	2176.81	1.44
Dependants	-345.06	-1.46
Educ. [Primary]	-1818.39	-1.40
Educ. [Above Primary]	772.00	1.00
Expenditure	5.20E-05	0.47
Membership	517.97	0.43
R-squared	0.14	N = 100

Table 6.7b Regression Results for Households Willingness to Pay for Private Radio: Brong Ahafo Region

Variable	Coefficient	t-Statistic
Constant	-2858.64	-0.38
Age [Up to 20]	5539.66	0.47
Age [Above 20]	2660.99	0.30
Married	2910.21	0.36
Dependants	-1189.75	-1.09
Educ. [Primary]	13947.68	2.58
Educ. [Above Primary]	15004.62	4.39
Expenditure	0.0025	2.16
Membership	3165.97	0.52
R-squared	0.27	N = 100

Table 6.7c Regression Results for Households Willingness to Pay for Extension Agent: Brong Ahafo Region

Variable	Coefficient	t-Statistic
Constant	6693.78	2.88
Age [Up to 20]	12995.18	1.08
Age [Above 20]	3495.19	1.42
Married	339.78	0.11
Dependants	-1556.88	-2.18
Educ. [Primary]	-200.056	-0.063
Educ. [Above Primary]	-4440.85	-1.22
Expenditure	0.0023	4.81
Membership	2655.38	0.76
R-squared	0.44	N = 100

CENTRAL REGION

Tables 6.8a, 6.8b, and 6.8c summarize the results for women's willingness to pay for information delivered via community radio, private radio, and by an extension agent. The explanatory power of the regressions is low, between 13% and 20%. There is no discernable pattern in the coefficient estimates for this region. For example, while household expenditure is the statistically significant factor in explaining the willingness to pay for information delivered via community radio, the significant factors explaining the willingness to pay for private radio are age and educational levels. Both the *above age 20* variable and *above primary* education variables are statistically significant at the 5% levels. The expenditure variable under community radio is significant at the 5% level, while the *above primary* education variable is significant at the 10% level. The results also show that the married women are willing to pay for information delivered via an extension agent with a 5% statistical significance. Since extension agents usually conduct workshops for groups rather than to individuals, it is surprising that membership in community organizations had a negative influence on women's willingness to pay for information delivered via extension agents.

Table 6.8a: Regression Results for Households Willingness to Pay for Community Radio: Central Region

Variable	Coefficient	t-Statistic
Constant	1751.18	3.19
Age [Up to 20]	-568.79	-1.09
Age [Above 20]	452.11	1.19
Married	289.20	0.98
Dependants	-43.98	-0.75
Educ. [Primary]	-86.45	-0.21
Educ. [Above Primary]	684.01	1.91
Expenditure	6.22E-05	2.31
Membership	-0.47	-0.00
R-squared	0.18	N = 100

Table 6.8b: Regression Results for Households Willingness to Pay for Private Radio:Central Region

Variable	Coefficient	t-Statistic
Constant	8797.45	1.59
Age [Up to 20]	-4358.46	-0.88
Age [20 and above]	10535.07	2.31
Married	978.85	0.49
Dependents	874.22	1.65
Educ. [Primary]	1347.16	0.41
Educ. [Above Primary]	7273.34	2.29
Expenditure	-0.00014	-0.80
Membership	-2838.95	-1.19
R-squared	0.20	N = 100

Table 6.8c: Regression Results for Households Willingness to Pay for Extension Agent Central Region

Variable	Coefficient	t-Statistic
Constant	6274.64	1.82
Age [Up to 20]	-6821.64	-1.81
Age [Above 20]	600.42	0.34
Married	4748.54	2.98
Dependants	-782.75	-1.42
Educ. [Primary]	2073.40	0.56
Educ. [Above Primary]	7502.87	2.40
Expenditure	0.00034	1.31
Membership	-3698.81	-1.84
R-squared	0.13	N = 100

Source: Survey Data 2004/5

EASTERN REGION

Tables 6.9a, 6.9b, and 6.9c summarize the results for the Eastern Region. Even though the overall explanatory power of the regression (R-square = 30%) is acceptable for regression based on cross section data, the signs on coefficients and the statistical significance of variables are consistent with expectations in only a few cases. For example, the results show that women above 20 years of age are more willing to pay for information delivered via community radio. Given that older persons are more likely to be members of community organizations, this is a plausible outcome. However, the estimate on the community organization variable is not statistically significant. The results also show that women with a large number of dependents are more willing to pay for information delivered via community radio, probably due to the lower cost of the community radio technology. Table 6.9b shows that older women are more willing to pay for information delivered via private radio (significant at 5% level), while younger women are less willing to obtain information via private radio. Rural women are willing to pay for information via private radio if they are educated, as shown by the statistically significant (5% level) results found for 'education above primary' variable in the table. The very low R-square (10%) reported in Table 6.9c and the statistically insignificant results found on variables make it difficult to draw any firm conclusions about the relationship between the factors examined in this study and rural women's willingness to pay for information delivered via extension agents in the Eastern region of Ghana.

Table 6.9a Regression Results for Households Willingness to Pay for Community Radio: Eastern Region

Variable	Coefficient	t-Statistic
Constant	2665.74	3.29
Age [Up to 20]	-268.57	-0.33
Age [Above 20]	2196.93	3.41
Married	93.68	0.13
Dependant	687.26	3.37
Educ. [Primary]	-245.65	-0.35
Educ [Above Primary]	-385.70	-0.60
Expenditure	-0.00018	-3.10
Membership	-468.77	-0.65
R-squared	0.30	N = 100

Table 6.9b Regression Results for Households Willingness to Pay for Private Radio:Eastern Region

Variable	Coefficient	t-Statistic
Constant	18106.83	6.65
Age [Up to 20]	-7741.15	-3.18
Age [Above 20]	6081.09	2.26
Married	-1579.73	-0.67
Dependants	332.81	1.22
Educ. [Primary]	2698.31	1.70
Educ. [Above Primary]	4235.39	2.08
Expenditure	-0.00	-1.02
Membership	-876.72	-0.50
R-squared	0.24	N = 100

Table 6.9c Regression Results for Households Willingness to Pay for Extension Agent: Eastern Region

Variable	Coefficient	t-Statistic
Constant	7446.89	5.61
Age [Up to 20]	-3583.77	-2.34
Age [Above 20]	552.36	0.35
Married	668.29	0.54
Dependants	162.98	1.37
Educ. [Primary]	-375.48	-0.50
Educ. [Above Primary]	-42.02	-0.07
Expenditure	3.40E-05	0.51
Membership	-326.04	-0.47
R-squared	0.10	N = 100

Source: Survey Data 2004/5

GREATER ACCRA REGION

All three regression equations (Tables 6.9a, 6.9b, and 6.9c) estimated for the Greater Accra Region yielded very low R-squares (13%), thereby making the explanatory power of the regressions very weak. Interestingly, the results for the Greater Accra Region reveal a consistency in the relationship between income and women's willingness to pay for information delivered via any of the three technologies. In all three cases, the proxy for income is statistically significant at the 5% level. Furthermore, the results show that educated households are more willing to pay for information delivered via a private radio or an extension agent (10% level of significance). The results for the willingness to pay for information via community radio are quite interesting, since they are contrary to what was obtained for the other regions. For the Greater Accra Region, younger women (below twenty years of age) are more willing to pay for information delivered via community radio (5% level), and also when the number of dependents is large (5%).

A plausible explanation for this outcome is as follows: the Greater Accra Region is a more urbanized region where one finds considerable numbers of youth programs designed especially to address issues of urban poverty. It may well be that the significant coefficient for the *below twenty* variable is capturing this youth effect. It may also be the case that the high cost of living in these urban-impact rural areas makes women who have a large number of dependents more willing to pay for information delivered via community radio, as it is the cheapest information delivery technology examined in this study.

GREATER ACCRA REGION

Table 6.9a Regression Results for Households Willingness to Pay for Community Radio: Greater Accra Region

Variable	Coefficient	t-Statistic
Constant	2785.18	6.10
Age [Up to 20]	1002.97	2.66
Age [Above 20]	248.82	0.89
Married	63.817	0.27
Dependants	103.07	2.19
Educ. [Primary]	44.57	0.17
Educ. [Above Primary]	-30.12	-0.15
Expenditure	3.34E-05	2.19
Membership	-329.51	-1.44
R-squared	0.13	

Table 6.9b Regression Results for Households Willingness to Pay for Private
Radio: Greater Accra Region

Variable	Coefficient	t-Statistic
Constant	13399.44	4.68
Age [Up to 20]	5352.52	1.22
Age [Above 20]	-813.63	-0.34
Married	2727.96	1.18
Dependants	354.42	0.69
Educ. [Primary]	2091.77	0.83
Educ.[Above Primary]	3175.58	1.68
Expenditure	0.00035	2.20
Membership	-2272.74	-1.03
R-squared	0.14	N = 100

Table 6.9c Regression Results for Households Willingness to Pay for Extension
Agent: Greater Accra Region

Variable	Coefficient	t-Statistic
Constant	6051.91	5.17
Age [Up to 20]	41.61	0.04
Age [Above 20]	-844.26	-1.06
Married	216.41	0.28
Dependants	200.41	1.04
Educ. [Primary]	762.70	1.08
Educ. [Above Primary]	1121.74	1.50
Expenditure	0.00	2.54
Membership	-204.13	-0.27
R-squared	0.13	N = 100

Source: Survey Data 2004/5

VOLTA REGION

Table 5.10a summarizes the effect of the selected factors on households'
willingness to pay for information delivered via community radio in the Volta
Region of Ghana. The overall explanatory power of the model as measured by
the R-square (Coefficient of determination) is much higher than the results from
other regions. Most of the signs on coefficients are as expected. Younger women
(below age 20) are less willing to pay for information via a community radio
(10% significance), while older women (above age 20) will be willing to pay for
information delivered via community radio. The estimated coefficient is statistically significant at the 5% level. All educated women in the Volta region are
willing to pay for information delivered via community radio, an outcome that is
not surprising given the very high number of educated women from the region.

The results also show that women who are members of a community organization will be willing to pay for information delivered via a community radio, at a 5% level of statistical significance.

Table 6.10b reports on women's willingness to pay for information delivered via private radio and follow the pattern observed for community radio. Older women are willing to pay for private radio (5% level of significance). Also, women with above primary school education show a strong willingness to pay for information delivered via private radio (1% level of significance). As in the case of community radio, women who are members of a community organization are willing to pay for information delivered via private radio. A similar pattern of responses is found in the results for the willingness to pay for information delivered through extension agents (Table 19c). Older women with above primary school education who are members of a community organization are willing to pay for information delivered via extension agents. The estimated coefficient for the above 20 age group, above primary education, and membership is all statistically significant at the 5% level.

Table 6.10a. Regression Results for Households Willingness to Pay for Community Radio: Volta Region

Variable	Coefficient	t-Statistic
Constant	1457.09	3.46
Age [Up to 20]	-832.28	-1.97
Age [Above 20]	753.60	2.10
Married	148.49	0.50
Educ. [Primary]	1116.60	2.45
Educ. [Above Primary]	1246.72	5.00
Expenditure	-2.51E-05	-1.30
Membership	933.78	2.95
R-squared	0.43	N = 100

Source: Survey Data 2005

Table 6.10b. Regression Results for Households Willingness to Pay for Private Radio: Volta Region

Variable	Coefficient	t-Statistic
Constant	-3700.46	-0.88
Age [Up to 20]	-1169.33	-0.35
Age [Above 20]	7122.12	2.92
Married	-1636.43	-0.77
Educ. [Primary]	3212.31	1.68
Educ. [Above Primary]	9092.74	5.01
Expenditure	0.00020	0.56
Membership	9599.48	3.60
R-squared	0.37	N = 100

Table 6.10c: Regression Results for Households Willingness to Pay for Extension Agent: Volta Region

Variable	Coefficient	t-Statistic
Constant	-2585.09	-0.63
Age [Up to 20]	1239.32	0.42
Age [Above 20]	4362.44	2.11
Married	-892.25	-0.67
Educ. [Primary]	1926.64	1.34
Educ. [Above Primary]	5519.84	4.65
Expenditure	0.00028	0.75
Membership	4710.06	2.42
R-squared	0.21	N=100

Source: Survey Data 2004/5

WESTERN REGION

Tables 6.11a, 6.11b, and 6.11c below summarize the results of the regression analysis for the Western region. The Tables show relatively higher R^2 for all the information media considered. The selected socio-economic factors explained about 26% of the variation in households' willingness to pay for information delivered via community radio, about 43% for the information delivered via private radio, and about 34% for the information delivered via extension agents. In addition to the relatively high explanatory power of the regressions, several of the important socio-economic factors hypothesized to influence households' willingness to pay for selected information media yielded consistent results. In all three regression models, there was a statistically significant relationship (1% and 5% levels) between willingness to pay and households with high education, high expenditure, and membership in community organizations. One result that does not lend itself to easy explanation is the relationship between marital status and the willingness to pay for information delivered via community radio. Table 6.11a shows that married households are not willing to pay for information delivered via community radio. This result is not corroborated by any other factors in the regression model, and hence it is difficult to explain. Generally, the regressions for the Western region contain valuable information for planning strategies to empower women in rural households in the Western region of Ghana.

Table 6.11a Regression Results for Households Willingness to Pay for Community Radio: Western Region

Variable	Coefficient	t-Statistic
Constant	-1483.62	-0.64
Age [up to 50]	3019.63	1.79
Married	-1839.23	-2.35
Dependents	291.01	0.48
Educ. [Primary]	-1486.95	-1.46
Educ. [Above primary]	1381.60	2.33
Expenditure	0.00065	3.38
Membership	1988.34	2.30
R-squared	0.26	N = 99

Table 6.11b Regression Results for Households Willingness to Pay for Private Radio: Western Region

Variable	Coefficient	t-Statistic
Constant	22.74	0.0066
Age [up to 50]	331.80	0.10
Married	-174.82	-0.084
Dependents	-892.45	-1.25
Educ. [Primary]	1012.20	0.60
Educ. [Above Primary]	6828.25	4.50
Expenditure	0.0011	3.63
Membership	7955.74	5.13
R-squared	0.43	N = 99

Table 6.11c Regression Results for Households Willingness to Pay for Extension Agent: Western Region

Variable	Coefficient	t-Statistic
Constant	994.14	0.63
Age [up to 50]	980.53	0.83
Married	32.53	0.037
Dependents	-79.56	-0.27
Educ. [Primary]	845.11	0.98
Educ. [Above Primary]	1794.91	3.17
Expenditure	0.00055	2.72
Membership	1971.61	2.27
R-squared	0.34	N= 99

Source: Survey Data 2004/5

UPPER WEST REGION

Table 6.12a summarizes the effect of the selected factors on households' willingness to pay for information delivered via community radio in the Upper West Region of Ghana. The overall explanatory power of the model as measured by the R-square (Coefficient of determination) is low (12%). Generally, R-squares obtained using cross-sectional data in statistical analysis tend to be low. The results show that older women (above 20 years) are willing to pay for information delivered via a community radio. This result is statistically significant at the 5% level. The results also show that women with more education (above primary level) are more willing to pay for information delivered via community radio. This result is also statistically significant at the 5% level. These outcomes are supported by the statistically significant (5% level) relationship between membership in a community organization and the willingness to pay for information delivered via a community radio.

Table 6.12b summarizes the results for households' willingness to pay for information via private radio. As in the case of the community radio, the overall explanatory power of the regression is low (11%), but the expected signs on coefficients are as expected. Using expenditure as an income proxy, the results show that women with high incomes are more willing to pay for information delivered via private radio, and the result is significant at the 5% level. Membership in community organizations is also statistically significant at the 10% level. As expected, women with a large number of dependents are not willing to pay for private radios, as indicated by the negative sign on the coefficient, even though the result is only mildly significant at the 10% level.

Table 6.12c summarizes the results for the willingness to pay for information delivered via an extension agent and the results are generally consistent with expectations. Women with more education are more willing to pay for information delivered via extension services. This result is statistically significant at the 5% level. In addition, membership in a community organization is statistically significant, also at the 5% level. The overall conclusion one can draw is that education and membership in a community organization are important factors in explaining rural women's' willingness to pay for information delivered via community radio and extension agents, while income is a critical factor in influencing willingness to pay for private radio.

Table 6.12a Regression Results for Households' Willingness to Pay for Community Radio:Upper West Region

Variable	Coefficient	t-Statistic
Constant	3613.51	2.54
Age [Above 20]	2025.88	2.44
Married	340.65	0.31
Dependants	-104.32	-0.76
Educ. [Above Primary]	3279.19	4.14
Expenditure	-0.00	-1.42
Membership	4089.84	3.92
R-squared	0.12	

Table 6.12b Regression Results for Households' Willingness to Pay for Private Radio: Upper West Region

Variable	Coefficient	t-Statistic
Constant	13459.55	1.96
Age [Above 20]	-10601.27	-1.55
Married	6814.89	1.39
Dependants	-631.28	-1.52
Educ. [Above primary]	-1709.22	-0.76
Expenditure	0.01	2.16
Membership	13384.25	1.92
R-squared	0.11	

Table 6.12c Regression Results for Households Willingness to Pay for Extension Agent: Upper West Region

Variable	Coefficient	t-Statistic
Constant	7219.27	6.98
Age [Above 20]	1021.40	1.19
Married	-100.99	-0.16
Dependants	-91.24	-1.23
Educ. [Above primary]	1189.61	3.53
Expenditure	-0.00	-0.97
Membership	3225.93	3.42
R-squared	0.16	

Source: Survey Data, 2005

UPPER EAST REGION

As in the case of the Upper West Region (Tables 6.13a, 6.13b, and 6.13c), the overall explanatory power of the regression for the Upper East Region is low. The highest R-square is 19%. Again there are no major surprises given that cross-sectional data is being used in the regressions. There appears to be a consistent pattern in the results for this region in the sense that income seems to be the driving factor for the willingness to pay for information delivered via the three technologies under consideration in this thesis. In all cases, income is statistically significant at the 5% level. The results also show that, as expected, women with a large number of dependents are less likely to pay for information technologies. The theoretical exploration suggested that large households spend more on food and the basic necessities of life, especially on health and shelter. It is not surprising that in all the technologies examined, there is a negative relationship between the number of dependents and households' willingness to pay for information. In all cases the estimated coefficient is significant at the 10% level.

Table 6.13a Regression Results for Households Willingness to Pay for Community Radio: Upper East Region

Variable	Coefficient	t-Statistic
Constant	2644.48	5.60
Age	597.10	1.67
Marital Status	-51.419	-0.17
No. of Dependents	-159.88	-3.01
Educ. [Primary]	-339.16	-1.04
Educ. [Above Primary]	-188.24	-0.67
Expenditure	0.000012	2.66
Membership	257.79	0.99
R-squared	0.16	(N) = 100

Table 6.13b Regression Results for Households Willingness to Pay for Private Radio: Upper East Region

Variable	Coefficient	t-Statistic
Constant	11718.43	2.87
Age [Up to 20]	1203.67	0.46
Age [Above 20]	2738.82	0.97
Marital Status	1422.34	0.52
No. of Dependants	-763.68	-1.94
Educ. [Above Primary]	2107.70	0.76
Expenditure	0.0014	2.96
Membership	3785.22	1.58
R-squared	0.19	

Table 6.13c Regression Results for Households Willingness to Pay for Extension Agent: Upper East Region

Variable	Coefficient	t-Statistic
Constant	5633.82	3.82
Age [above 20]	1910.57	1.66
Married	-184.53	-0.20
Dependants	-266.84	-1.84
Educ. [Primary]	-604.51	-0.61
Educ. [Above Primary]	66.42	0.07
Expenditure	0.00042	2.95
Membership	1180.72	1.73
R-squared	0.18	

Source: Survey Data, 2005

NORTHERN REGION

The summary of regression results for the Northern Region of Ghana is shown in Table 6.14a, 6.14b, and 6.14c. As in the case of the other regions, the explanatory power of the model is quite low (between 7% and 17%). The signs and statistical significance of most of the factors are not consistent with expectations. Probably the strongest factor is membership in a community organization, which is statistically significant and consistent with expectations in the case of women's willingness to pay for information delivered via community radio. Table 6.14a shows that married women are not willing to pay for information delivered via community radio. There could be several reasons explaining this result, the most plausible being the cost of maintaining a two-person versus one-person household. Consistent with expectation, the results show that women who are members of a community organization are willing to pay for information delivered via community radio (Table 6.14a).

The results show that younger women (below age 20) are willing to pay for information delivered via private radio. The estimated coefficient is significant at the 5% level (Table 6.14b). This group is not willing to pay for information delivered via an extension agent, an outcome that is statistically significant at the 10% level (Table 6.14c). Women who have above primary school education are willing to pay for information delivered by an extension agent, an outcome that is statistically significant at the 5% level (Table 6.14c).

Table 6.14a: Regression Results for Households Willingness to Pay for Community Radio: Northern Region

Variable	Coefficient	t-Statistic
Constant	3653.83	15.48
Age [Up to 20]	-320.01	-1.13
Age [Above 20]	-24.78	-0.18
Married	-567.79	-3.26
Dependants	-49.76	-0.87
Education [Above Primary]	-556.64	-1.48
Expenditure	4.61E-05	0.85
Membership	510.81	2.17
R-squared	0.14	N = 100

Table 6.14b Regression Results for Households Willingness to Pay for Private Radio: Northern Region

Variable	Coefficient	t-Statistic
Constant	22601.71	9.23
Age[Up to 20]	5275.66	2.82
Age [Above 20]	-49.36	-0.045
Married	1858.81	1.16
Dependants	126.23	0.49
Educ. [Above Primary]	1468.45	0.85
Expenditure	0.00047	1.83
Membership	906.08	0.68
R-squared	0.076	N = 100

Table 6.14c: Regression Results for Households Willingness to Pay for Extension Agent: Northern Region

Variable	Coefficient	t-Statistic
Constant	6140.82	7.89
Age [Up to 20]	-2376.81	-1.99
Age [Above 20]	4.65	0.0082
Married	-0.25	-0.00038
Dependants	78.27	0.86
Educ. [Above primary]	5038.58	2.19
Expenditure	-8.85E-05	-1.44
Membership	600.94	1.38
R-squared	0.17	N = 100

SUMMARY

- In summary it could be emphasized that there appeared to be variations in the results obtained from all the regions.
- Being a cross-sectional study, the overall explanatory power of the model was poor, with an R^2 of 7.5% for the community radio regression, 6.9% for private radio, and 8.4% for extension.
- The overall results of the pooled data revealed consistency and statistical significance of most of the critical socio-economic factors that were hypothesized to influence rural women's' willingness to pay for selected information delivery media.
- The results showed that older women (above 20 years of age), educated above the primary school level, with high expenditure levels, who are members of a community organization, are more willing to pay for information delivered via a community radio.
- Married women were willing to pay for information delivered via private radio.
- Table 10a shows that younger women (below age 20) were not willing to pay for information delivered via a community radio.
- With the exception of the income factor, statistically significant at the 10% level, all the other factors were significant at the 1% and 5% levels.
- A similar pattern prevailed for information delivery via extension agents. Similarly, the principal factors were high education, high expenditures, membership in community organizations, age, and marital status.
- The only factor that was not found significant in explaining variation in the choice of information media was the number of dependents.

12

ASSESSING WILLINGNESS TO PAY FOR INFORMATION DELIVERY: DISCUSSION OF REGRESSION RESULTS

INTRODUCTION

This chapter discusses the results of the analysis of the field data as presented in the previous chapter. From the regression results of the pooled data and the regional results, one could make the following deductions:

1. Typical of a cross-sectional study, the overall explanatory power of the model was poor, with an R^2 of 7.5% for the community radio regression, 6.9% for private radio, and 8.4% for extension agents.
2. The overall results of the pooled data revealed consistency and statistical significance of most of the critical socio-economic factors that were hypothesized to influence rural women's' willingness to pay for selected information delivery media.
3. The results revealed that older women (above age 20), educated above the primary school level, with high expenditure levels, who are members of a community organization, are more willing to pay for information delivered via a community radio.
4. Married women were willing to pay for information delivered via private radio.
5. Younger women (below age 20) were not willing to pay for information delivered via a community radio.
6. Concerning willingness to pay for information delivery via community radio, with the exception of the income factor that was statistically significant at the 10% level, all the other factors was significant at the 1% and 5% levels.

7. Similarly, concerning information delivery via extension agents, the principal factors were high education, high expenditures, membership in community organizations, age, and marital status.
8. The only factor that was not found significant in explaining variation in the choice of information media was the number of dependents.

These key findings raise a number of issues on the relationship between the socio-economic factors and one's willingness to pay for information delivery.

RESULTS FROM POOLED DATA OF ALL REGIONS

1. Age

It was hypothesized that older households would be more willing to pay for community radio systems and extension visits. Among the reasons for this was that older female household's heads were likely to belong to community organizations and hence were more comfortable with sharing the media. On the other hand, young female household heads were also likely to be less involved in community organizations, and would be willing to pay for their own private radio system. This confronted us with the questions:

1. Will older female household heads be more willing to pay for community radio systems?
2. Will younger households heads be willing to pay for private radio systems?

From the results (Tables 6.5a, b, c), it was found that the older women were willing to pay for information delivered via a community radio or via extension services, but not via private radio. The high significance of the community membership variable (1%) may explain why the older population prefers information via community radio or extension services. It is likely that the older population may be members of community organizations. Conversely, younger women were generally unwilling to pay for information delivered via any of the suggested technologies.

Though the age factor was not statistically significant in explaining the willingness to pay for information by rural women, it is very important in planning an effective program to deliver information to rural households using ICT, the reason being that even though this factor was not statistically significant, it had the right signs consistent with the hypothesis. In addition, a very high percentage (94%) of the respondents fell within the active adult stage of 21 to 50 years (Table 6.1). These people could be described as being in their peak stage of development and production. Their responses could well inform policy in the use of ICT for rural adult education and willingness to pay for such facilities and services. And as expressed by Kusi-Nkrumah (2004), adults may have several reasons for continuing learning. Furthermore, the distribution points to a need to examine education program content and the relevance of the information delivered.

2. Marriage

It was hypothesized that married women were likely to be more willing to pay for private radio media. The reason for this assertion was that married women were more confined to private life. Several socio-cultural factors affected their level of participation in public life and their interaction with strangers. In addition, child care, home care, and other domestic activities form the priority of (rural) married women's engagements, and these limit their ability to engage in leisure and other empowering socio-economic activities. Limited by these inhibiting factors, they were likely to prefer to have their own private radios. Another contributing factor to married women's willingness to pay for private radios could be that married women could have higher income (spouses combined income) and could therefore afford the more expensive media for information delivery. The question for investigation then became, *Are married women likely to be more willing to pay for private radio media?*

The pooled results found the marital status of rural women to be statistically significant in explaining the variation in the willingness to pay for information delivered via private radio (1% level; Table 6.5b), and through extension services (10% level; Table 6.5c). Even though the marital status variable had the correct sign under the community radio regression (Table 6.5a), the variable was not statistically significant.

This presents us with some policy implications. The survey indicated that a majority of nearly 70% of the household heads were married (Fig. 6.1), pointing to an important socio-cultural factor that must be taken into account in planning information delivery to rural women via ICT. Men occupy a dominant role in Ghanaian society, and this dominance is even more pronounced in rural communities. The existent roles and status of women/wives, and the nature of the male-female relationship in these communities, place considerable burden on women's time allocation. A more comprehensive rural education program must therefore take into account this dominant position of men (Adoo-Adeku 2004; Awumbila 2001). Thus their views, consent and support would be crucial for effective program planning and implementation.

3. Household Size

The household was defined to include all persons who were under the direct responsibility of the female household heads. At a given income level, large households were less likely to pay for private radios, given the cost of these radios. Thus, the hypothesis was that large households will be more willing to pay for community radios and extension services, while small households were more likely to be willing to pay for private radios. This presented us with the following question: *Are large households more willing to pay for community radios?*

From the field data, the pooled results did not find the number of dependents of rural women to be statistically significant in explaining the variation in households' willingness to pay for information under any of the regressions in the model. The estimates under community radio had the correct negative sign for the number of dependents variable, but the variable was woefully statistically insignificant.

It might be observed that, while it is typical of a rural Ghanaian household to report as many as 17 dependents within a household, the survey found the majority of the respondents (88.3%) to have dependents ranging from 0 to age 6 (Table 6.2). A further breakdown showed that over 55% had the total number of their dependents ranging from 0 to 3, which suggests that a good number of households may not have the huge financial burden associated with maintaining a large number of dependents. In planning ICT information delivery to rural women, holistic planning dictates that the government take a long-term view of the empowerment process and include issues related to population planning, which on the surface seem like a remote factors.

4. Education

In the fight against poverty, Figure 6.2 reveals the need to focus on rural female education. Rural females were observed to have lower school attendance rates across all regions, with the lowest rates recorded in the three northern regions (Northern, Upper West and Upper East). It was hypothesised that educated households will be willing to pay for any ICT media, given the premium on information in decision-making. While an illiterate household naturally would depend on the radio and extension visits for information, a literate household had the additional source of information delivered through extension bulletins and other printed sources. The question then became: *Will educated women be more willing to pay for information media?*

While there were nontrivial regional variations, the overall results from the study pointed to household education as one of the principal factors influencing rural women's willingness to pay for the various technologies used in information delivery to women in rural areas. The results from the pooled data found education to be significant at the 5% level.

The significance of the education factor supports the need to plan and implement ICT policies for rural empowerment in a holistic context. Education is one of the major components of Ghana's poverty reduction program and the MDG. The survey results show that in its effort to empower rural women using ICT to deliver information, the government has a major hurdle to clear. Formal educational attainment appears to be very low among the female rural household heads. The survey showed that about 45% of the household heads had no formal education, and that only 1.1% had attained tertiary education. Thus, even though rural women who had some education had expressed a strong willingness to pay for information, considering Oduro-Mensah's (2004, 4) expression that "all education is purposive and designed to achieve an end," policy and program planners have to undertake *specially designed* adult education programs to benefit rural women. The results likewise imply that information would have to be delivered to rural households in a language they understand and in a medium with which they would be comfortable. The significance of the education variable also points to a need to emphasize *local content* when designing rural information programs (Dzakpasu 2000; Oduro-Mensah 2001; Siabe-Mensah 2003; Amedzro 2005).

5. Income

It was difficult to predict the effect of income on the willingness to pay for ICT in rural households. Generally, a positive relationship between income and the willingness to pay for ICT was expected. Households with high incomes tend to spend a smaller proportion of income on food, while poorer households spend a higher proportion of income on food (Table 6.3). Thus, one expected the effect of income on ICT to be positive in the relatively richer regions. Furthermore, one expected households with high incomes to use private radios instead of community radios in receiving information.

One could also argue that even though poorer households spend a higher proportion of income on food, their interest in obtaining information to *jump-start* out of poverty could encourage them to be willing to pay for ICT information. In essence, there were no statistically significant differences in households' willingness to pay across regions. In this sense, it was difficult to predict the exact sign (positive or negative) on the income variable, and the issue was left to empirical determination. An indirect approach was used to obtain measures of income from rural households. Households were first asked to list their major sources of income, and then asked about their expenditure patterns due to the difficulty in obtaining direct income figures from households and capture the effect of transfers. These expenditure amounts were used as proxies for income. The GLSS found that only about 13% of rural dwellers maintained a savings account, thus the expenditure figures were a plausible measure of household financial situation in a given year. Indeed, studies of willingness to pay for amenities in rural households have found direct rural income measures to be unreliable and have thus resorted to proxies to estimate income (Boadu 1989). The guiding question for investigation was therefore framed as: *Are households with high income willing to pay for information media?*

Like the education variable, the overall results (Tables 6.5 a, b, c) from this study pointed to household expenditures (used as proxy for income) as one of the principal factors influencing rural women's willingness to pay for the various technologies used in information delivery to women in rural areas. The results from the pooled data found income to be significant at 10%.

These results point to a need to cast rural empowerment policies and programs within the broader poverty reduction policies of the government, and within the attainment of the Millennium Development Goals (MDG's). As defined under its *Vision 2020* goal, Ghana's primary poverty reduction objective is to become a middle-income country by the year 2020. The results show how the attainment of this vision would boost ICT-use in delivering information to rural households, since income was found to be consistently statistically significant in explaining rural women's willingness to pay for information.

There are two important issues to address in the context of the relationship between incomes and ICT-use to empower rural women. First, the relationship between ICT-use and income must be seen as bi-directional. While high incomes make it possible for rural women to pay for the information delivery technology of choice, the delivered information, in turn, is intended to empower women to be able to make those decisions that would improve their welfare and incomes. These bi-directional effects are captured in the analysis by providing a feedback loop in the theoretical framework (Fig. 5.1) that emphasizes the importance of *learning* in the empowerment process. These observations lead to the conclusion that knowledge of the importance of incomes in ICT-use in information delivery is simply not enough. To further improve their incomes, there is a need to emphasize the learning component that allows rural women to better utilize received information in decision-making.

A second implication of the statistical significance of the income factor is the need to broaden policies to enhance the many possible sources of income available to rural women. Even though the popular view has been to focus on agriculture as the primary source of raising incomes of rural women, the survey results point to a need to broaden the scope of an income policy in rural areas. The field survey results (Table 6.3) showed that the majority of women (45.8%) reported trading as the primary source of income; 23.9% reported farming; 7.7%, dressmaking; 4.1%, 2.7%, 2.6% reported hairdressing, teaching, and office work, respectively, as the primary source of income. A sizable percentage (11.2%) reported no income source.

The distribution of women's sources of income is beginning to put flesh on some of the results obtained in the study. For example, the distribution may help explain why several households were not willing to pay for information delivered by extension agents, since their historical mission is the delivery of agriculture-related information. The results may also explain the popularity of private radio because radios may complement such activities as hairdressing, dressmaking, office work and trading. Key for policy and program planners is to better understand the dynamics of the rural sector and recognize shifts in economic activity that may be counter to the historical pattern of economic activity.

6. Membership in Community Organizations

It was hypothesized that households belonging to community organizations will be willing to pay for information delivered via community radio. Community radio was estimated to be less costly than a private radio, and, more importantly, these households had cultivated the spirit of sharing through their membership in an organization. GLSS 4 data (Table 5.2) showed that rural households make more contribution to community initiatives than do urban households. By analogy, it was hypothesized that households in the more deprived areas (especially in the northern regions) will be more willing to pay for community radio and extension services compared to those rural communities located near the urbanized regions such as Accra, Kumasi (Ashanti), Takoradi (Western), Cape Coast (Central). This presented us with the question: *Will households belonging to community organizations be willing to pay for community radio systems?*

Similar to the results on the education and income variables, membership in community organizations also emerged as a principal factor in influencing rural women's willingness to pay for the various technologies used in information delivery to women in rural areas. The results from the pooled data (Tables 13a, b, c) show that membership in a community organization is significant at 1% level.

This statistical analyses point to an important role that community organizations could play in the delivery of information to empower rural women. Women who belong to some form of community organization were more willing to pay for information delivered via the three ICT media examined in the study. The survey showed that slightly more than half (50.3%) of rural women belonged to a community organization and cooperative. This strong sense of communalism has important policy and program planning implications. For example, to reduce costs and hence be able to extend programs to cover a larger population group, the government may want to take advantage of the spirit of communalism and focus on programs that could be delivered to a group. It also means that there is a need to design effective feedback mechanisms, because in a group context it may not be possible to easily address individual concerns. Information program content may emphasize discussion as a way to sustain group interest. In order to check practices such as free riding and shirking, it is important for development workers and government to allow rural organizations to define their own rules. Attempts by government agents to interfere in group organization could be counterproductive.

REGIONAL RESULTS

The results based on regional data followed the pattern observed under the pooled results. With the notable exception of the Volta and Upper West regions, the income variable was found to be statistically significant in explaining the variation in the willingness to pay for information delivered under the selected media for all the other regions.

The education variable was found to be statistically significant for all regions except the Northern, Greater Accra, and Upper East regions, while the community membership variable was found to be statistically significant in all regions (for at least one of the media), except in the Ashanti, Brong Ahafo, and Eastern regions.

The only regions where the age variable was not found to be significant in explaining the variation in willingness to pay for any media were Western, Ashanti, and the Upper East. Likewise, the number of dependents variable yielded inconclusive results.

Unlike the outcome using the pooled data, the marital status of women did not play a significant role in explaining the willingness to pay for any of the regions.

SUMMARY

It could be emphasized that while there were nontrivial regional variations, the overall results from this study point to household expenditures (used as proxy for income), household education, and membership in community organizations as the principal factors influencing rural women's willingness to pay for the various information delivery technologies to women in rural areas. The results from the pooled data found membership in a community organization, education, and income to be significant at the 1%, 5%, and 10% levels, respectively. Though the age, marriage and household size variables were not statistically significant in explaining the willingness to pay for information by rural women, they appeared to be very important in planning an effective delivery information program to rural households using ICT. The reason is that even though these factors were not statistically significant, their indicators were consistent with the hypothesis.

13

POLICY IMPLICATIONS FOR USING ICT'S AND ADULT EDUCATION FOR EMPOWERMENT OF RURAL WOMEN

OVERVIEW

The study reported in Chapter Twelve used rural household survey data (collected from all the ten administrative regions in Ghana) to examine rural women's willingness to pay for information delivered via three technologies: community radio, private radio, and extension agents. The primary objective of this study was to identify the critical factors to consider in the planning and policy design in using ICT to provide information to empower rural women. Literature survey was used to identify the key factors that have been identified by other authors as important in designing ICT policy in a developing-country context. The identified factors were used in designing a survey instrument that was administered in face-to-face interviews with selected rural women in Ghana. The data from the survey were used in a linear regression model to obtain quantitative estimates of the impact of the identified socio-economic factors on households' willingness to pay for the three information delivery technologies: *community radio, private radio, and extension agents*. The regression model was first estimated using the data from each of the ten administrative regions. The data were combined, and a single model estimate was undertaken using the pooled data.

The need to examine ICT-use in adult education for empowering rural women within a holistic context is the overriding conclusion of this study. In the planning of policies, no single socio-economic factor emerged as the *magic bullet*, and no programs to introduce ICT-use in information delivery to rural women emerged. Likewise, no single information delivery technology emerged as *the technology* to use in delivering information to rural women.

SUMMARY OF FINDINGS

Pooled Results

Education, income and community membership: While there were nontrivial regional variations, the overall results from this study point to household expenditures (used as proxy for income), household education, and membership in community organizations as the principal factors influencing rural women's willingness to pay for the various technologies used in information delivery. The results from the pooled data found membership in a community organization, education, and income to be significant at the 1%, 5%, and 10% levels, respectively.

Age: It was found that the older women were willing to pay for information delivered via a community radio or via extension services, but not via private radio. The high significance of the community membership variable may explain why the older population prefers information via community radio or extension services. It is likely that the older population may be members of community organizations. Disturbingly, younger women were generally not willing to pay for information delivered via *any* of the suggested technologies.

Marriage: The pooled results showed the marital status of rural women to be statistically significant in explaining the variation in the willingness to pay for information delivered via private radio (1% level), and through extension services (10% level). Even though the marital status variable had the correct sign under the community radio regression, the variable was not statistically significant.

Household size: The pooled results did not find the number of dependents of rural women to be statistically significant in explaining the variation in households' willingness to pay for information under any of the regressions in the model. The estimates under community radio had the correct negative sign for the number of dependents variable, but the variable was statistically insignificant.

REGIONAL RESULTS

Based on regional data, the results follow the pattern observed under the pooled results. With the notable exception for the Volta and Upper West regions, the income variable was found to be statistically significant in explaining the variation in the willingness to pay for information delivered under the selected media for all the other regions. The education variable was found to be statistically significant for all regions except the Northern, Greater Accra, and Upper East regions, while the community membership variable was found to be statistically significant in all regions for at least one of the media, except in the Ashanti, Brong Ahafo, and Eastern regions. The only regions where the age variable was not found to be significant in explaining the variation in willingness to pay for any media were Western, Ashanti, and the Upper East. Likewise, the number of dependents variable yielded inconclusive results. Unlike the outcome using the pooled data, the marital status of women did not play a significant role in explaining the willingness to pay for any of the regions.

Despite the lack of consistency in the regression results obtained using the pooled as against the regional data, several important policies and planning options could be proposed from the results of this study.

POLICY IMPLICATIONS

1. Need to Disaggregate Policy Planning and Implementation Process

Even though the government sets the overall national ICT policy, the results from this study suggest some merit in allocating considerable authority to regional and local authorities in setting priorities and approaches to empowering rural women through the use of ICT. This is due to the different impacts the socio-economic factors had on different regions. It is in this context that the government must put *teeth* into the Local government Act (1988) PNDC Law 207. The instructions under Article 35 Ghana's 1992 constitution state that the "State will make democracy a reality by decentralizing the administration and financial machinery of government to regions and districts and by providing all possible opportunities to the people to participate in decision making at every level of national life and in government."

Government has made some efforts to broaden the participation of strategic groups in the public policy and planning decision-making process, as evidenced in the preparation of Ghana's Poverty Reduction Program (GPRP). For example, the GPRP planning group consulted 36 community groups during the preparation of the document, including women, youth, and community leaders (GPRS 2003, 6). To obtain their input in preparing the strategy paper, the planning group held seminars with women and leaders of women's groups, a coalition of which prepared a statement listing the areas which they felt had not been treated as part of the first draft document. Following this workshop, NETRIGHT engaged a consultant to prepare inputs into the GPRS in order to make it more *gender sensitive* (GPRP 2003, 7). While these initiatives are laudable, the study results point to a need to deepen this consultation process with even greater emphasis on local control and input from women.

2. Need to Implement ICT Policy within a Broader Poverty Reduction Program

A. Improving Rural Incomes

The study results also point to a need to cast rural empowerment policies and programs within the broader poverty reduction policies of the government, and within the attainment of the Millennium Development Goals (MDGs). As defined under its *Vision 2020* goal, Ghana's primary poverty-reduction objective is to become a middle-income country by the year 2020. The results show how the attainment of this vision would boost ICT-use in delivering information to rural households, because income was found to be consistently statistically significant in explaining rural women's willingness to pay for information. In the context of the relationship between incomes and ICT-use to empower rural women, there are two important issues to address.

First, the relationship between ICT-use and income must be seen as bi-directional. While high incomes make it possible for rural women to pay for the information delivery technology of choice, the information delivered is in turn intended to empower women to be able to make those decisions that would improve their welfare and incomes. These bi-directional effects are captured in the analysis by providing a *feedback loop* that (in the theoretical framework's empowerment process) emphasizes the importance of *learning*. Thus the *information content* must be designed to advance women's skills and elevate their status in ways that advance their decision-making powers and thus improve their incomes.

Secondly, an implication of the statistical significance of the income factor is the need to broaden policies to enhance the many possible sources of income available to rural women. Even though the popular view has been to focus on agriculture as the primary source of raising the income level of rural women, the survey results point to a need to broaden the scope of income policy in rural areas. The field survey results show that the majority of women (45.8%) reported trading as the primary source of income, while 23.9% reported farming as their primary source. About 7.7% reported dressmaking as their primary source of income; 4.1%, 2.7%, and 2.6% reported hairdressing, teaching, and office work, respectively, as their primary source. A sizable percentage (11.2%) reported no income source.

The distribution of women's sources of income is beginning to put flesh on some of the results obtained in the study. For example, since the historical mission of these agents is the delivery of *agriculture-related* information, the distribution of which may help explain why several households were not willing to pay for information delivered by extension agents. The results may also explain the popularity of private radio, considering that radios may complement such activities as hairdressing, dressmaking, office work and trading. The key for policy and program planners is to better understand the dynamics in the rural sector and to recognize shifts in economic activity which may be counter to the historical pattern of economic activity.

B. Education

Education emerged as another important factor in explaining households' willingness to pay for information. The significance of the education factor supports the need to plan and implement ICT policies for rural empowerment in a holistic context. Education is one of the major components of Ghana's poverty reduction program and the MDG. The survey results show that the government has a major hurdle to clear in its effort to empower rural women using ICT to deliver information. Formal educational attainment appears to be very low among the female rural household heads. The survey showed that about 45% of the household heads had no formal education. Only 1.1% had attained tertiary education. Thus, even though rural women who had some education had expressed a strong willingness to pay for information, policy and program planners have to undertake *specially designed* adult education programs to benefit rural women. The results also indicate that information would have to be delivered in a language they understand and in a medium with which they are comfortable. The significance of the education variable also points to a need to emphasize *local content* when designing rural information programs.

C. Community Organizations

Regarding information delivery, the statistical analysis also points to an important role that community organizations could play to empower rural women. Women who belong to some form of community organization are more willing to pay for information delivered via the three ICT media examined in the study. The survey showed that slightly more than half (50.3%) of rural women belonged to either a community organization or a cooperative. This strong sense of communalism has important policy and program planning implications. For example, the government may want to take advantage of the spirit of communalism and focus on programs that could be delivered to a group as a way to reduce costs, and hence be able to extend programs to cover a larger population group. It also means that there is a need to design effective feedback mechanisms, because in a group context it may not be possible to easily address individual concerns. Information program content may emphasize discussion as a way to sustain group interest. It is important for the government to allow rural organizations to define their own rules to check practices such as *free riding* and *shirking*. Attempts by government agents to interfere in group organization may be counterproductive.

D. The Need to Develop a Disaggregated Funding Strategy

In addition to disaggregating the policy and planning process in using ICT to provide information to rural women, the results also point to a need to formulate policies and programs in such a way as to prevent duplication of efforts. This study has helped to identify factors that influence rural women's willingness to pay for different information delivery technologies. The many factors have different effects in different regions. This opens the door for policy and program planners to *allocate efforts* among different agencies and development partners.

The survey showed that rural women were very interested in receiving information. About 49.7% responded in the affirmative when asked whether they received information on agriculture, trading, health, education, and government. A higher percentage (72.5%) indicated their desire to acquire information and skills, and this is a good indicator for the need for a *specially designed* rural adult program for the women. Only 7.6% responded that they pay for information delivery. On the other hand, 77.6% indicated their willingness to pay for the learning media if the government was to offer such a specially designed program, and 4.8% could not decide. In a similar vein, 79.3% indicated their willingness to pay for such a facility if offered by a private organization. While a large majority of the respondents said they believe that it is the responsibility of the individuals using the facility to pay for information, a few indicated that the government, the District Assemblies, or NGO's should pay for the information. To be able to target information delivery programs that will reach the appropriate rural population, policy and program planners must take into account both the needs of individual regions and the alternative funding sources available.

E. Need for Holistic Planning

Several factors surfaced that, while not statistically significant in explaining the willingness to pay for information, nevertheless are important, and (consistent with the hypothesis) these factors need to be built into any ICT information delivery planning program. One of these factors is age. Consider: a very high percentage (about 94%) of the respondents fell within the active adult stage (age 21 to 50) and could be described to be in their peak stage of development and production. Their responses could well inform policy on the use of ICT for rural adult education as well as willingness to pay for such facility and services. Furthermore, the distribution points to a need to examine education program content and the relevance of the information delivered. Additionally, it is clear that the education program content and the relevance of the information delivered are of great import.

The number of dependents in a household is another important factor. It was hypothesized that women with many dependents would be less willing to pay for information, given the cost in maintaining a large household. For the purpose of this study, the term *dependents* is not limited to the biological daughters and sons of respondents, but includes their wards and any other people for whom they are responsible. While it is typical of a rural Ghanaian household to report as many as 17 dependents within a household, the survey found the majority of the respondents (88.3%) to have dependents ranging in number from 0 to 6. A further break-down showed that over 55% had a total number of dependents ranging from 0 to 3. This suggests that a good number of households may not have the huge financial burden associated with maintaining a large number of dependents. *Holistic planning* dictates that the government take a long-term view of the empowerment process, which would include issues related to population planning that, on the surface, seem like remote factors in planning ICT information delivery, and yet may influence the results of empowerment policies or programs.

Another seemingly remote factor is the marital status of rural women. The survey indicated that a majority (almost 70%) of the household heads were married and points to an important socio-cultural factor that must be taken into account in planning ICT information delivery. Men occupy a dominant role in Ghanaian society, and this dominance is even more pronounced in rural communities. The existing roles and status of women/wives and the nature of the male/female relationship in these communities place a considerable burden on women's time allocation. A more comprehensive rural education program must therefore take into account this dominant position of men. Thus their views, consent and support would be crucial for effective program planning and implementation.

F. Need for the Critical Political Will

To advance the empowerment process of its rural women, the Government of Ghana has, through various policy pronouncements and position papers, expressed its commitment to provide information through the use of ICT. Government's commitment however must be examined within the broader context of the allocation of budgetary resources to rural education programs and ICT development. As noted earlier, over 70% of government ministries spend less than 10% of their budgets on ICT-related activities. With the global trend towards e–government, government may want to signal its commitment by increasing its own use of ICT. Furthermore, several indicators point to the possibility of significantly expanding ICT use for information delivery, to empower rural women, and the following is an examination of several of these indicators.

Ghana already has an extensive telecommunications network that reaches every region in the country (Fig. 5.3). Given the strong expression of willingness to pay for information delivered via community radio, private radio and extension services, the government may need to explore ways of *strengthening the existing network* to achieve its goal of empowering rural women through ICT information delivery.

Ghana's considerable experience in rural education programs should reduce the learning curve to a significant degree. In an effort to inform and entertain the rural people in regional languages, Rural Broadcasting (RB) began in October,

1962, with programs designed to educate both men and women. In programs designed to stress dignity in labour, segments targeting farmers and fishermen consisted of agricultural news; interviews with successful farmers; talks by experts on new methods of farming; nutrition; and child-care and market reports. To determine the extent to which the listeners practiced their trade using the new knowledge and skills discussed in the radio program, broadcasting staff followed up with visits. One dimension of the RB programs explained by Abbey-Mensah (2001) was the Rural Radio Forums, introduced in 1964; groups of farmers met at a central location to listen to special radio programs on improved methods of farming, after which they discussed the content of the program with onsite agriculture extension officers. Recognizing the roles rural women play in housekeeping, farming, preservation, and the selling of agricultural products, a special 30-minute daily program was broadcast for the rural women. Other initiatives include the *Worsum* Clubs, radio forums organized by the School of Communication Studies of the University of Ghana, which appear to be making a significant impact on the income-generating activities of the rural people. In the effort to achieve the goal of empowering rural women, there is a continuing need to build on these proven activities.

There are currently several available technologies that avoid many of the technical constraints (especially the absence of electricity) that prevent the introduction of popular technologies such as computers. For example, wind up and solar powered radios may be operated directly by spring-generated power or by using solar panels. The *Freeplay Global Shortwave Radio*, which weighs 5 lbs. 51 oz. / 2.5kg, has no need for batteries or external electrical power sources. The *Freeplay Radio* plays all day in direct sunlight, and when low-light conditions prevail it automatically switches over to spring power (if the radio has been previously wound). For convenience, the *Freeplay* may also be powered using AC/DC 6 Volt wall adapters and the radio has been distributed to refugee camps in Burundi and in Tanzania's Great Lakes region. Another innovative product that could help improve the community radio program is the *Suitcase Radio* product, developed by a Canadian company, Wantok Enterprises (www.wantokent.com). Both its radio and television systems were designed for use in areas where infrastructure such as roads and power grids are either nonexistent or in very limited supply; everything operates from 13.8 Volts (a fully charged car battery voltage); solar panels, wind generators, standard gasoline or diesel chargers can also charge the batteries. If AC power is available, the company supplies an AC to DC power supply that will convert 230 Volts to 13.8 Volts DC. The company has community radio stations in many African countries and in the Caribbean, Asia and, to a lesser extent, Eastern Europe. Most of their radio stations are in Niger (75 or 80 units) and Mali (45). Niger (one of the poorest countries in the world), has 90% of its equipment running on solar-charged systems. The discussion of emerging technologies illustrates the importance of strategic planning as a process, with frequent updating based on new information.

G. Need for Inter-Agency Coordination

In any massive government program, two of the most difficult hurdles are minimizing turf battles and waste and achieving effective coordination. An ICT program to deliver information to rural women would involve technical experts, policy planners, and several public and private agencies. And at minimum such a program should include the Ministries of Finance, Education, and Agriculture, local government, and science and technology. At the agency level, one could think of the Ghana News Agency (GNA), the extension service, and the Institute of Adult Education. To these must be added the numerous NGO's and bilateral agencies that are pursuing their own development aid activities consistent with their national priorities. The challenge for government will be to coordinate these many institutions to optimize resources devoted to rural adult education.

One option is to create a *super agency,* one that draws personnel from the various agencies with the specific single objective to *supervise* ICT activities directed at rural communities. Such an agency could serve as a *clearinghouse,* a one-stop shop for all activities connected with rural information delivery. There is no doubt that adoption of these proposals will enhance the use of information and communication technology to reach the unreached in society ... *our rural women*!

REFERENCES

Abbey-Mensah. 2001. *Expert consultation on rural women and distance learning: Regional Strategies.* <http://www.fao.org/sd/ 2003/PE12033a_en.htm http://www.fao.org/sd/ruralradio/en/index.html> (DA: 11/12/04).

"Adult Education and Poverty Reduction: A Global Priority." 2004. *The Gaborone Statement and Recommendations for Action.* <http://www. aepr.co.bw/aepr/html/aepr.htm> (DA: 07/07/05).

Advocates for Gender Equity (AGE) *Report on Mapping, Exercise on Gender Activities in Ghana.* 2000. Accra.

Adupa, Joyce. 2001. *Desk Study on the Existing Infrastructure for Providing Agricultural Information to Farmers and Sources of this Information.* Electronic Delivery of Agricultural Information to Rural Communities in Uganda.

Addo-Adeku, K. 1989. *An Action Plan for a Community Education Programme in the Ga District.* Institute of Adult Education. University of Ghana: Legon.

Adu, J.I. 1999. *Woman in Human Development.* Accra: Horizon Publications. *Agenda for the Future – Six Years Later.* 2003. *ICAE Report.* <http://www .icae.org.uy/> (DA: 05/05/05).

Akinpelu, J. A. 2002. *Philosophy and Adult Education.* Lagos: Stirling-Horden Publishers.

Alaluusua, Seppo. 1992. *Cost Analysis and Pricing in Distance Education.* 1:15-30.

Alima, Mahama. 2001. *Gender Training for Development Planners: Training Experience in Tsikata.* In *Gender Training in Ghana.* Accra: Woeli Publishing Services.

Amedzro, A. K. 2004. In *The Practice of Adult Education in Ghana,* edited by Asiedu, et al. al. Accra: Ghana Universities Press.

Amedzro, D. K. 2005. Globalization: Non-Formal Education and Rural Development. Accra: Ghana Universities Press.

Amedzro, A. D. K. 2005. *Theory and Practice of Community Education.* Accra: Ghana Universities Press.

Annan, Kofi. 2002. UN General Assembly.

Ardayfio-Schandorf E. 1991. *Household Headship and Female Earning in Ghana.* In *Family and Development in Ghana.* Edited by Ardayfio-Schandorf. Accra: Ghana Universities Press.

Asante, E.K. 1978. Changing *Status of the Wife in Dormaa Ahenkro.* A project work submitted to the Department of Sociology, University of Ghana, Legon.

Awumbila, M. 2001. *Women and Gender Equality in Ghana: a Situational Analysis.* In *Gender Training In Ghana – Politics, Issues and Tools.* Edited by Dsikata, D. Ghana: Woeli Publishing Services.

Balit, S. 1999. *Rural Women and Communication.* In *Voices for Change* <http://www.fao.org/docrep/x.2550e/X2550e03.htm.> (DA 23/03/06).

Bangkok, Thailand. 2000. *Expert Consultation on Distance Learning Resources for Rural Women.* From the FAO Corporate Document Repository. <http://www.fao.org/documents/> (DA: 01/04/05).

Bartel, P.J.W. 1978. *Modernization and the Decline in Women's Status.* From Proceedings of the Seminar of Ghanaian Women in Development, volume II.

Benneh, G. 1996. *Women's Access to Agricultural Land in the Household.* In *The Changing Family in Ghana.* Edited by Ardayfio-Schandorf. Ghana: Ghana Universities Press.

Boadu, F.O. 1993. *Contingent Valuation for Household Water in Rural Ghana.* Journal of Economics, 43(3).

Boatema, B. 2001. *Training Women's Groups and their Leaders.* In *Gender Training in Ghana.* Edited by Tsikata. Accra: Woeli Publishing Services.

Bukh, J. 1979. *The Village Women in Ghana.* Uppsala: Scandinavian Institute of African Studies.

Bhola, H.S. 1980. *Why Literacy Can't Wait in Issues for the 1980's. Convergence.* XIV (1).

Bortei-Doku, Ellen. *A note on Theoretical Directions in Gender Relations and the Status of Women in Africa.* In a *Gender Analysis Workshop Report.*

Brown, C.K. 1996. *Decision-making in Ghana.* In *The Changing Family in Ghana.* Edited by Ardayfio-Schandorf. Accra: Accra Universities Press.

Cabral, I. 1995. *Achieving Women's Empowerment. Convergence* XXVIII (3): 45-51.

Carlo, M. S. and S.E. Sylvester.1996. *Adult Second-Language Reading Research: How May It Inform Assessment.* <http://www.literacyonline.org/products/ncal/pdf/TR9608.pdf> (DA: 01/01/05).

Campbell and Katona. 1966. The Sample Survey. In *Research Methods in the Behavioural Sciences.* Edited by Festinger and Katz. New York. Holt, Rineholt and Winston.

Carolyn, M. 1997. *Promoting the Empowerment of Women through Adult Learning. Adult Education and Development.* DVV(49): 81-90.

Colverson, K.E. 1995. *Case Studies of Women's Needs for Agricultural Programming.* Convergence. XXVIII (3): 36-44.

Cragg, C.E.; Andrusyszyn, M. A.; and Humbert, J. 1999. *Experience with Technology and Preferences for Distance Education Delivery Methods in a Nurse Practitioner Program.* <http://cade.athabascau.ca/vol14.1/cragg_et _al.html> (DA: 12/16/04).

Cross, K.P. 1981. *Adults as Learners: Increasing Participation and Facilitating Learning.* California: Jossey-Boss.

Coldevin, Gary. 2003. *Participatory Communication: A Key to Rural Learning Systems.*<http://www.fao.org/sd/2003/KN10023_en.htm>

Conference Reports.1949; 1960; 1972; 1976; 1985; and 2004. International Conference of Adult Education. <http://www.icae.org.uy/ > (DA: 05/05/05.

Curran, Chris. 1989. *Resource Factors: Recurrent Costs.* In *UNESCO and International Council for Distance Education, Developments in Distance Education in Asia: An Analysis of Five Case Studies.* 32-37.

Dawson, Elsa.1998. *Assessing the Impact: NGOs and Empowerment.* In *Women and Empowerment.* Edited by Afshar Haleh. New York: St. Martin's Press Inc.

Dede, Chris. 2004. *Planning for "Neomillennial" Learning Styles: Implications for Investments in Technology and Faculty.* < http://icommons.harvard.edu /~gse-> (DA: 11/09/04).

Dede, C. 2004. *Enabling Distributed-Learning Communities via Emerging Technologies.* From *Proceedings of the 2004 Conference of the Society for Information Technology in Teacher Education (SITE),* Charlottesville, VA: American Association for Computers in Education. <http://icommons.harvard.edu/~gse-> (DA: 11/09/04).

Defnitions.www.unesco.org/education/educprog/lwf/doc/portfolio/defiNitions.ht m> (DA: 05/05/05).

Diane, Elson. 2000. *Targets and Indicators: Selection from Progress of the World's Women.* UNIFEM.

Dinucci, Alessandro and F. Zeremariam. 2003. *Understanding the Indigenous Knowledge and Information Systems of Pastoralists in Eritrea* <http://www.fao.org/sd/2003/KN11013en.htm> (DA: 12/10/04).

Dolphyne, A. Florence. 1991. *The Emancipation of Women: An African Perspective.* Ghana: Ghana Universities Press.

Durkheim, E. 1956. *Education and Sociology:* Illinois: The Face Press.

Dzakpasu, C. C. K. 2000. *Traditional Adult Education in Puberty and Nugbetor. Ghana Journal of Literacy and Adult Education.* 2(1).

Ellis, P. 1995. *Non-Formal Education and Empowerment of Women. Convergence.* XXVIII (3): 86-90.

Empowerment. UNESCO. <www.unesco.org/education/educprog/lwf/doc/ portfolio/definitions.htm> (DA: 5/05/05).

FAO. 1996. *Expert Consultation on Extension Rural Youth Programmes and Sustainable Development.* <http://www.fao.org/docrep/w1765e/w1765e00 .htm> (DA: 2/3/03).

FAO. 2005. *Take Action: Raise awareness of the Contribution of Rural Women in the United States to Small Towns, Communities, and Agriculture. Rural Women Zone.* <http://www.ruralwomyn.net/report_one.html> (DA: 3/23/06).

FAO. 2002. <http://www.fao.org/documents/ > (DA: 12/17/04).

FAO Rural Radio and Simbani. < http://www.simbani.amarc.org/ > (DA: 11/18/04).

Fontaine, Gary. 2002. *Presence in "Teleland."* In Handbook of Online Learning – Innovatins in Higher Education and Corporate Training. Edited by Redestam, Schoenholtz and Read. London: Sage Publications.

Ghana. 2003. *Ghana Poverty Reduction Strategy 2003 -2005: An Agenda for Growth and Prosperity.* <http://www.usaid.gov/pubs/cbj2003/afr/gh/> (DA: 02/08/2005).

Ghana. 1992. *Constitution of the Republic of Ghana.* < http://www.idlo.int /texts/leg5515.pdf> (DA: 09/16/04).

Ghana. 2000. *Ghana Living Standards Survey (GLSS) 4, 2000.*

Ghana Poverty Reduction Strategy, 2003 -2005: An Agenda for Growth and Prosperity, February 2003. <http://poverty.worldbank.org/files/Ghana_ PRSP.pdf > (DA: 09/16/04).

Ghana National ICT Policy and Plan Development Committee. <http://www. ict.gov.gh/html/about.html> (DA: 11/20/04).

Ghana Vision 2020. < http://www.ghana.edu.gh/prospects/vision.html> (DA: 10/15/04).

Girard, Bruce. 2003. *The Challenges of ICT's and Rural Radio.* Expert Consultation on Rural Women and Distance Learning: Regional Strategies. <http://www.fao.org/sd/2003/PE12033aen.htm> (DA: 12/10/04).

Greenstreet, M. 1978. *Social Change and Ghanaian Women. Canadian Journal of African Studies.* VI. (2): 351-55.

Group, W. B. 2005. Project Information Document (RIP): 4.

Heng, C.L. 1995. *Women's Empowerment. Convergence.* XXVIII (3): 78-85.

Holmes, Rebecca. 2004. Advancing Rural Women's Empowerment: Information and Communication Technologies (ICTs) in the service of Good Governance, Democratic Practice and Development for Rural Women in Africa. *A Women's Net Resource Paper* <http://womensnet.org.za/dimitra_ conference/papers.shtml> (DA: 11/11/04).

Ilboudo, Jean-Pierre. 2001. *Rural Radio: Role and Use over the Past Three Decades.* <http://www.fao.org/documents/show_cdr.asp?url_file=/docrep/ 003/x6721e/x6721e02. htm > (DA: 12/10/04).

ICAE Strategic Plan, 2003 – 2006. <http://www.icae.org.uy/> (DA: 05/05/05).

ICT4D: Connecting People for a Better World – Lessons, Innovations and Perspectives of Information and Communication Technologies in Development. <http://www.globalknowledge.org/ict4d/index.cfm?menuid=43>.

Information and Communication Technologies Servicing Rural Radio: Final report of the International Workshop. 2003. <http://www.fao.org/sd /2001/KN1102_en.htm>

International Literacy Institute. 2002. *Towards the Guidelines for the Improvement of Literacy Assessment in Developing Countries: Conceptual Dimensions Based on the LAP Project, Working Document of the International Literacy Institute.* <http://www.literacy.org/products/ili/pdf/LAPGuidelines .pdf> (DA: 01/01/05).

ITU (International Telecommunication Union), Africa. 2003. *ICT Indicators, 2003.*http://www.itu.int/ITU-D/ict/statistics/at_glance/af_ictindicators .html (DA 11/20/04).

Jarvis, C. 1995. *Empowerment Through Popular Culture. Convergence.* XXVIII (3):72-76.

Jones, M. L. 1995. *Phonics in ESL Literacy Instruction: Functional or Not?* <http://www.literacyonline.org/products/ili/pdf/ilprocmj.pdf>   (DA: 01/01/05).

Kamara, S. 2001. *The Journey of a Male Gender Trainer in Northern Ghana.* In *Gender Training in Ghana.* Edited by Tsikata. Accra: Woeli Publishing Services.

Karen, Evans. 1995. *Barriers to Participation of Women in Technological Education and the Role of Distance Education.* <http://www.col.org/ barriers.htm>.

Karl, Marilee.1995. *Women and Empowerment: Participation and Decisionmaking.* London: Zed Books Ltd.

Kelly, Burton, et al. 1994. *Researching Women's Lives and Studying Women's Oppression.* In Researching Women's Life from Feminist Perspective. Edited by Maynard and Purvis. London: Taylor and Francis.

Kumekpor, T.K.B. 1999. *Research Methods and Techniques of Social Research.* Ghana: Sonlife Press Services.

Kipuri, N.O. 1991. *The Impact of Development on the Roles of Pastoral Women.* In Culture, Gender, Science and Technology in Africa. Edited by K.K. Prah. Namibia: Harp Publications.

Kwapong, O. T. F. 2005. *Using Adult Education for Empowerment of Rural Women. Adult Education and Development.* 65: 135 - 152.

Lephoto, M.H. 1995. *Educating Women for Empowerment in Lesotho.* Convergence XVIII (3): 5-10.

Manu, T. 1984. *Law and the Status of Women in Ghana.* Paper prepared for the UN Economic Commission for Africa.

Manuh, T. 1998. *Africa Recovery Briefing Paper - Women in Africa's Development - Overcoming Obstacles, Pushing for Progress. Africa Recovery.* Vol. DOI.

Moser, Caroline O.N. 1993. *Gender Planning and Development: Theory Practice and Training.* London: Routledge.

Malcom, K. S. 1980. *The Modern Practice of Adult Education – From Peda-gogy to Andragogy.* Chicago: Follet Publishing Company.

Marclay. 2001. <http://edevelopment.media.mit.edu/SARI/papers/pae.ksg.pdf > (DA: 2/10/04).

McLean, Scott and Dirk Morrison. 2000. *Sociodemographic Characteristics of Learners and Participation in Computer Conferencing.* <http://cade. athabascau.ca/vol15.2/mclean.html> (DA: 12/16/04).

Miliband, David. 2003. *Teaching in the 21st Century - Speech to the Centenary North of England Education Conference.* <http://www.findarticles. com/p/articles/mi_go1633/is_200301/ai_n6500392> (DA: 2/01/04).

Muhammad, Yunus. *Grameen Bank – Bangladesh Bridging the Digital Divide.* <www.grameen.com>; <www.grameen.org>; <http://www.microcredit summit.org/press/grameen.htm> (DA: 10/17/04).

Microsoft Encarta Reference Library. 2005. *Microsoft Corporation.*

Millennium Development Goals. <http://www.un.org/millenniumgoals/ > (DA: 10/21/2004).

MOWAC. 2005. *Strategic Implementation Plan 2005 – 2008.* Ministries of Women and Children's Affair, Ghana.

National ICT Policy and Plan Development Committee, Republic of Ghana. 2004. <http://www.ict.gov.gh/html/Landscape%20of%20ICT%20Human%20Resourc es%20&%20Expertise%20.htm> (DA 02/19/2005).

Nath, Vikas. 2001. *Empowerment and Governance through Information and Communication Technologies: women's perspective.* <http://www.cddc.vt .edu/knownet/articles/womenandICT.htm> (DA: 11/02/04).

NCWD. 1994. *The status of Women in Ghana. National Report for the 4th World Conference on Women.* Accra.

NETRIGHT. 2004. *Ghana NGO Alternative Report for Beijing + 10 (FINAL VERSION,* Network for Women's Rights in Ghana (NETRIGHT). <http://www.wildaf-ao.org/eng/IMG/doc/Ghana_ENG-2.doc> (DA 02/08/ 2005).

NFED. 2005. *Non-Formal Education Division – Celebration of International Literacy Day. Daily Graphic of Ghana,* September 9th 2005.

Nikoi, Gloria. 1999. *Gender and Development.* Ghana: Ghana Universities Press.

Nukunya, G.K. 1969. *Kinship and Marriage Among the Anlo-Ewe.* New York: The Athleme Press.

Obeng-Darko, E. 1999. Womanhood. Ghana: Journagraft.

Oduro, A.D. 1992. *Women's Economic roles" in Gender Analysis Workshop Report.* Legon.

Oduro-Mensah, D. 2001. *Towards the Promotion of Adult Science Education in Developing Countries. Legon Journal of Humanities.* XII: 148.

Ofei-Aboagye, E. 2000. *Promoting the Participation of Women in Local Governance and Development: The Case of Ghana.* ECDPM Discussion Paper18. Maastricht: ECDPM.

Ollennu and Avokey. 2000. *Coping With Single Parenting.* Accra: Asempa Publishers.

Oppenheim, A.N. 1972. *Questionnaire Design and Attitude Measurement.* London: Heinemann Educational Books Ltd.

Oppong, C. 1967. *Husbands and Household Work: A Ghanaian Ethnic Variation.* Legon Institute of African Studies.

Oppong, C. 1970. *Conjugal Power and Resources: An Urban African Example.* *Journal of Marriage and the Family* 32(4): 76-680.

Oppong, C. 1974 Middle *Class African Marriage.* London: George Allen and Urwin.

Oppong, C. 1974. *Marriage Among a Matrilineal Elite.* Legon Institute of African Studies.

Oppong, C. 1974. *Domestic Rights and Duties in Southern Ghana.* *Legon Family Research Papers*, No.1. Legon Institute of African Studies.

Oppong, C. 1974. *Female and Male in West Africa.* London. George Allen and Unwin.

Oppong, C. and Abu, K. 1987. *Seven Roles of Women: Impact of Education, Migration and Employment on Ghanaian Women.* Geneva: ILO.

PACT NEPAL. *Women's Empowerment Project (WEP) Literacy and Micro credit - Creating Opportunities.* <www.pactworld.org; <http://www.microcreditsummit.org/press/PACT.htm>

Paolucci, B, et al. 1977. *Family Decision-making: An Ecosystem Approach.* New York: John Wiley and Sons.

Perraton, Hilary. 2000. *Open and Distance Learning in the Developing World.* Routledge: London.

Phoenix. 1994. "Practising Feminist Research: The Intersection of Gender and 'Race' in the Research Process." In *Researching Women's Life from Feminist Perspective.* Edited by Maynard and Purvis. London: Taylor and Francis.

Quadir, I. Z. 2000. *Connecting Bangladeshi Villages.* <http://www. devmedia.org/documents/ACF1055%2Ehtm>; <http://www.telecommons.com/villagephone/quadir.html>
<http://www.grameen-info.org/grameen/gtelecom/ > (DA: 10/17/04).

Rattray, R.S. 1929. *Ashanti Law and Constitution.* Oxford: Oxford University Press.

Riel, Margaret. 2000. *New Design for Connected Teaching and Learning.* <http://www.gse.uci.edu/mriel/whitepaper/learning.html>.

Roberts, P. 1991. "Anthropological Perspectives on the Household." *IDS Bulletin.* 22 (1): 60-66.

Robertson, C. 1990. "Ga Women and Socio-economic Change in Accra, Ghana." In *Women in Africa*. Edited by N.J. Hafkin and E.G. Day. California: Stanford University Press.

Roncoli, M. 1985. "Women and Small-scale Farming in Ghana." *Women in International Development Working Paper Series*. Michigan: Michigan State University Press.

"Report on Mapping, Exercise on Gender Activities in Ghana." 2000. Advocates for Gender Equity (AGE). Accra.

Rowlands, J.O. 1998. "A Word of the Times, but What Does it Mean? Empowerment in the Discourse and Practice of Development." In *Women and Empowerment: Illustrations from the Third World*. Edited by Afshar Haleh. New York: St. Martin's Press, Inc.

Rudestam, Schoenholtz and Read, editors. 2002. *Handbook of Online Learning – Innovations in Higher Education and Corporate Training*. London: Sage Publications.

Rumble, Greville. 1997. *A Basic Framework for Analysing Revenue Costs*. <http://wbweb4.worldbank.org/DistEd/Management/Benefits/fore-01.html> (DA: 12/10/04).

Russell, Mary and Lynda Ginsburg. 1999. *Learning Online: Extending the Meaning of Community. A Review of Three Programs From the Southeastern   United   States.* <http://literacyonline.org/products/ncal/pdf/TR9901.pdf> (DA: 01/01/05).

Sabatini, John. 2001. *Designing Multimedia Learning Systems for Adult Learners: Basic   Skills   With   a   Workforce   Emphasis.* <http://www.literacy.org/products/ncal/pdf/WP0001.pdf> (DA: 01/01/05).

Sanyal, B. C. 2001. *New Functions of Higher Education and ICT to Achieve Education for All*. <http://www.literacy.org/products/ili/pdf/UTLPsanyal .pdf> (DA: 01/01/05).

Sarumi, A. 2001. *Contemporary Issues in Historical Foundations of Adult Education*. Ibadan: D-GAI Publishers.

Schalkwyk. 1997. "Concepts and Approaches to Gender Equality." *DAC Sourcebook*. <http://www.oecd.org/dac/htm/sourcebk.htm>.

Scott, S.M. et al. 1995. "Participation for Empowerment. *Convergence*. XXVIII (3): Pgs.63-70.

Seini, W. 2004. Environmental Services Provided by Selected Farming Systems in Ghana. Accra: ISSER.

Sen, A. 1984. *Resources, Values and Development*. Oxford: Blackwell.

Shapiro, J. J. & Hughes, S. K. 2002. *"*The Case of the Inflammatory E-Mail: Building Culture and Community in Online Academic Environments.*"* In *Handbook of Online Learning – Innovations in Higher Education and Corporate Training*. Edited by Rudestam, et al. London: Sage Publications.

Siabe-Mensah, R. A. A. a. K. 2003. *Literacy: A Key to Development*. Accra: Ghana Universities Press.

Sibanda, Jennifer. 2001. *Improving Access to Rural Radio by 'Hard-to-Reach' Women Audiences.*

Smith, H.W. 1975. *Strategies of Social Research.* London: Prentice Hall, Inc.

Stack, E.K. et al. 1995. "Credit with Education: A self-Financing Way to Empower Women. *Convergence.* XXVIII (3): 26-30.

Stamp, P. 1989. "Technology, Gender and Power in Africa." Technical Study 63e, IDRC, Ottawa.

Strategic Plan of the International Council of Adult Education (ICAE).2003-2006. *Agenda for the Future – Six Years Later.*

Subba, Rao. 2002. *Literacy Assessment Practices (LAP) in Selected Developing Countries: The Case of India.* < http://www.literacy.org/products /ili/pdf/LAPIndiaCase_total.pdf > (DA: 01/01/05).

Subedi, A. & Garforth, C. "Gender, Information and Communication networks: Implications for extension." *European Journal of Agricultural Education and Extension.* 3 (2).

Tevie, William. 2004. *The Ghana Experience with ICT Policy Development.* <http://216.239.57.104/search?q=cache:XBg5Cv_2550J:www.dosh.gm/confere nces/ict/gambia-undp.ppt+Ghana+ict+policy+document&hl=en > (DA: 11/20/04).

Tan, J. Lee, K.H., and A. Mingat. 1984. *User charges for Education: The ability and*

willingness to pay in Malawi. Staff Working Paper 661. Washington, D.C: The World Bank.

TECH21: *A National Technology Laboratory for Literacy and Adult Education.* <http://www.literacy.org/tech21.html>.

Thalhimer, Mark. 2000. *How Does Radio News Stack Up Against The Rest? RTNDF's American Radio News Audience Survey.* <http://www.rtndf .org/default.asp>.

Thobani, M. 1983. *Efficiency and equity implications of user charges in social sector service: The financing of education in Malawi.* Staff Working Paper 572, *Washington*, D.C: The World Bank.

Tsikata, D. 2001. "Gender Equality and Development in Ghana: Some Issues which should concern a Political Party." In *Gender Training in Ghana.* Edited by D.Tsikata. Accra: Woeli Publishing Services.

UN World Summit on the Information Society (WSIS), Geneva. 2003. <http://www.itu.int/wsis/> (DA: 10/20/04).

UN. 1995. "Improvement of the Situation of Women in Rural Areas." *General Assembly.* <http://www.un.org/documents/ga/res/50/a50r165.htm> (DA: 3/23/06).

UN. 2005a. "What rights for women as rural citizens? - Rural Women's Recommendations." *World Rural Women's Day.* <http://www.rural-womens-day.org/declaraEng05.html>. (DA: 3/23/06).

UN. 2005b. "Rural Women at the United Nations - Toward a Platform for Action for Rural Women: Emphasis on Health, Education and Work." *The 2nd Annual Women and the Arts Festival at the Commission on the Status of Women.* <http://www.ruraldevelopment.org/win05-06-ruralwomenatuni tednations.html>.

UN. 2006. "Economic Advancement for Women - Report of the Secretary-General." *Economic and Social Council.* E. a. S. C.-C. o. t. S. o. Women. Fiftieth Session.

UNESCO. 2001. " Improvement of the situation of women in rural areas." *Resolution Adopted by the General Assembly on the Report of the Third Committee, 88th Plenary Meeting.* <http://www.unescap.org/icstd/documents /resolutions/res%2056> (DA: 3/23/06).

UNFPA. 2005. *The Promise of Equality: Gender Equity, Reproductive Health and the MDGs. State of World Population.* T. A. Obaid.

UNFPA. 2005. State of the World Population 2005.

Valiukenas, D.J. 1987. *Writing with Authority: A guide to the Research Process.* New York: Random House, Inc.

Voices for Change: Rural Women and Communication.2003. <http://www.fao. org/sd/2003/KN0601_en.htm> (DA: June, 2003).

WARD. 2006. "A Background to the West African Situation: Where WARD Fits In." *West African Rural Development Centre.* <http://www.ward .gm/back.html> (DA: 3/23/06).

Wignaraja, P. 1990. *Women, Poverty and Resources.* New Delhi: Sage Publications.

Wagner, D. A. 2000. *EFA 2000 Thematic Study on Literacy and Adult Education.* <http://literacyonline.org/products/ili/pdf/OP0001.pdf> (DA: 01/01 /05).

Wagner, Dan and Robert Kozma. 2003. *New Technologies for Literacy and Adult Education: A Global Perspective – A Paper in Support of the UN Literacy Decade, he Education for All Initiative, World Summit on the Information Society and Leave No Child Behind.*

Waldick, Lisa. 2003. New Wireless Network for Uganda's Healthcare Workers.SATELLIFE: The Global Health Information Network (12/08/04).

Walter Fust in Waldburger & Weiger, eds. 2004. *ICT4D – Connecting People for a Better World – Lessons, Innovations and Perspectives of Information and Communication Technologies in Development.* <http://www. globalknowledge.org/ict4d/index.cfm?menuid=43> (DA: 12/04/05).

Wei, Meng Hong. 2002. *Literacy Assessment Practices (LAP) in Selected Developing Countries: The Case of China* <http://www.literacy.org/products /ili/pdf/LAPChinaCase_total.pdf> (DA: 01/01/05).

Westoff, Charles and Akinrola Bankole. 1997. *Impact Data - Accessing Mass Media on Reproductive Behavior – Africa.* < http://www.comminit.com /evaluations/idmay15/sld-2291.html> (DA: 12/10/05).

"Women in Public Life in Ghana." 1998. Research Report. ISSER/DPPC Research Team.

World Bank. 2003. *Development Data Group.*

World Summit on the Information Society (WSIS). 2003. <http://www.itu.int/wsis/> (DA: 05/05/05).

Yuan, F. 2003. "Awakening Rural Women's Potential." *China Daily.* <http ://www.china.org.cn/english/Life/54778.htm>. (DA: 1/30/03)

www.ingramcontent.com/pod-product-compliance
Lightning Source LLC
Chambersburg PA
CBHW051239050326
40689CB00007B/985